People are Clamoring a

"Stop contacting r
–**Salman Rushdie raves about Christina Oxenberg**

"Your submission has been reviewed and rejected."
–*The New Yorker*

"You're fucking who?"
–**Chelsea Handler**

"She's just the daughter of minor European royalty…"
–**Queen of England**

"That Bitch promised to write about me!"
–**Candace Bushnell**

"She's not Asian and she's not related to me, but I'd still fuck her."
–**Woody Allen**

"Wasn't there an Oxenberg on Dallas or Falcon Crest? Where is she now?"
–**Jay Leno**

1

Christina Oxenberg

Life is Short:
Read Short Stories

Table of Contents

Also by Christina Oxenberg

TAXI

Royal Blue

Do These Gloves Make My Ass Look Fat?

Will Write for Compliments

Life is Short:
Read Short Stories

for

Ashley

INTRODUCTION

WELCOME TO THE woolgathering. This slim tome is another year's worth of short stories gathered here for your entertainment. Most of them chronicle my passive-bystander adventures as a newcomer to this enchantingly fair isle of Key West, Florida. The theme of the stories revolve around my entranced and fawning worship for this gorgeous coral rock, and its denizens who find themselves misfits no longer in this tolerant, welcoming and creative community.

2011 ~ 2012 was mostly spent in Key West, but occasionally I was obliged to foray north, to my birthplace of New York City. Included in this collection is a single hat toss to my former foothold in the Hamptons with Authors Night. The stories are not in chronological order, as that would be dull. Instead they are as follows:

Sacrificial Leaf is a good place to begin with a reverential rendering of Mother Nature. **Amigo** conjures my imagination and may or may not resemble persons alive or dead, you will have to make that decision yourself. **Aunt Muriel** brilliantly conceals the true identities of a couple who would be mortified to have been found out; their secrets are safe with me. **Rainy Season** is a broad undefined stretch of time best observed from a durable structure. **Strip Club**, on the other hand, is best observed close by with a fistful of dollar bills. **Blood Orange** is a long suppressed memory from an incident I remember like it was yesterday. **Impromptu** was a moment in time I happened to witness and feel so lucky for it. **Downsize** is a true story and comes from the messy lives of a troubled couple laboring within the confines of tiny minds. **Tarts** is a soliloquy from one of my best friends, and that is as much of a clue as I shall provide, other than his name, Nalim. **Snakes on a Plane** is a firsthand account of mass hysteria, my own included.

Evan & Elle and Part II are my version of a fabled local 'urban myth' of a retired couple making the big move to Paradise, only they never arrive, for one reason or another. **Bum Fishing** is a real game, probably originating with Abbott and Costello or the likes, and makes for a good time had by all. **Afternoon** is what you see if you tool around the Coral Rock on any given day. **Jumble** is another fabulous rant from my friend Nalim, only he knows who he is. **Teamwork** is a sorry state of affairs for a very nasty couple I know; they are beyond redemption but great for fiction. **Tandem** is a story constructed from the paranoid weavings of my mind and may be one hundred percent accurate, equally it could be wildly incorrect; you decide. **Flora & Fauna** is a meditation on the garden at my current rental in Key West, filled with the awe I feel every day.

Away Game is a story inspired by a young man I met, as is often the case. **Home** is a story that jolted me into reality and forced me to take stock of my happy surroundings. **The Dancer** is an entrancing female who entertains on the streets of the city of Key West, and whenever I see her I have to stop and admire. **To Hell** is an exaggeration of an encounter I had with some milquetoasts, no offense intended. **Eden** perhaps is Karmic retribution and recounts my introduction to the rat snake, now a daily visitor through the garden of my current domicile. **Judo** recounts the impressions of a total novice to the wonderful world of martial arts, and its artists. **Card Sound Road** is a path to travel more, combining the delight of a roller coaster with a background of blissful splendor; try it, you'll like it.

On the Fly is my enforced departure from Key West, due to misjudging exactly when my rental would be available, requiring a trip north to New York City, and empty guest rooms, to sop up the errant spare time. **Party Crash** was a sordid reminder of why I left town in the first place.

Friends is a silent nod to my tolerant and forgiving hosts, all of them through the years. **Three Dog Night** says hello and goodbye to a tribe since dismantled; you figure it out. **End of an Era** was a funeral dressed up like a night at Studio 54, a fitting tribute after all. **Thank You & Happy New Year** can be skipped as they are my sycophantic love affair with anyone who reads me, apologies for the apple-polishing. **Nidification** is a reverie on the pros and cons of moving to Hoboken, NJ, and how I snapped out of it.

I Scream, Again is a throwback to *I Scream*, a story from my first compilation of short stories, titled *Do These Gloves Make My Ass Look Fat?* **Novak Djokovic** is Serbia's pride and joy, the tennis champion, and I love him!! **Peacocks** is weak but I needed it to help fill this book. **Off My Rocker** provides useful gauges by which to measure madness; help yourself. **Mosquito Season** is a great reason never to ask me if you can come stay. The final story, **Authors Night**, details one of my favorite events, the East Hampton Library fund raiser; I'll be back!

SACRIFICIAL LEAF

AN ORDINARY Thursday afternoon and a friend invited me on his boat. My friend's boat is a fashion model of elegance and femininity and five of us floated away on the pretty craft, mostly adrift in private worlds. I know I was. Even in Paradise reality can cast insidious shadows causing a partial eclipse of the soul.

From the marina we chugged beneath a bridge and then gathered speed over waters in jades and lime greens and all under a radiant sky. Careful wending through channels and cuts took us out to the Gulf of Mexico and an expanse of ocean dotted with faraway islands.

The boat motored smoothly and cooling spray doused us with baptismal purification. Long slim fish cut through the surface, slicing like so many knives, before vanishing in raucous splashes. Clearly visible were squads of barracudas tacking right and left, chasing tiny fish moving in masses of fast darting escape.

Approaching the shallows, the islands devolved into mere tangles of mangroves. Someone explained the history of these local mangroves, and their ritual of traveling as bobbing green sticks across stretches of sea, until they meet with a desired depth. Then they secure themselves, throwing down an anchor, gradually knitting a system of sticks that downward produce roots and upward generate limbs sprouting canoe shaped shiny green leaves. Except for the irregular yellow leaf which is dedicated to absorbing toxic salts from the seawater. The leaf will die and fall off, thus known as the sacrificial leaf.

We anchored before a half-moon beach. To a view of perfection, perfumed by a dense honeyed air, we lunched. Sated we ventured into the clear, cool water, each of us in different directions. I swam down into the silence and watched a manta ray emerge, upending the sandy seabed, waggling off into the wicked liquid.

Back on dry land we attempted an inland stroll which was cloyingly hot, and immediately I was sweating. Our trek soon ended when we met with man-eating insects and a swamp that welcomed our footsteps like a salivating mouth.

With mangroves up close you see the vulnerability; the negative space being wider than any supports, barely strong enough for the tiniest of birds to land within. Reminding me of people I have known who appear, from a distance, robust and independent; like islands.

On the return trip, perhaps it was the time of day and exactly how the late afternoon sunlight reflected but the mangrove islands, now black cylinders on the horizon, appeared to levitate above bars of glowing gold, shaped like space ships ready for takeoff. A cleansing occurs under the broiling sun. As with the photosynthesis of the mangroves, the salts of reality can collect and fall away, like teardrops. As we sped across calm ocean the sunset exploded with showy pinks and deepening oranges. With all my sensations tickled my equilibrium was restored and my appreciation in life renewed.

In Key West there is no such thing as an ordinary Thursday afternoon.

AMIGO MIGHT as well have been a cat. Every night at the restaurant it was the same, when the place filled up, Amigo speeding through a heedless throng, a heavy tray in his hands, held aloft. He never lost control of the tray no matter how heaped. All of him was slim and hard and he smoothly split a path through the crowd, a cat in the tall grass. He noticed the lady in the green dress. She was a regular and he always noticed her because something about her reminded him of his mother.

Later that evening Amigo was at a club with his friends but he recognized her the instant she entered. Paused in the entrance she looked like she wanted to bolt, like she was there on a dare. Until that moment he had forgotten all about her. He must have been in the back of the restaurant when she left because now that he thought about it he had not seen her leave. Had forgotten about her until this minute and now she was standing in the doorway of his salsa club. Without thinking he reached for the tattoo on his shoulder. The tattoo was the outline of his mother's hand.

Just like every Sunday after work Amigo was with his friends. In a huddle they cavorted until the music started and then they cruised around and

21

propositioned partners. Effortlessly Amigo crossed the room and materialized in front of the lady in the green dress. Wordlessly, gracefully he held out a hand.

"No! I can't dance!" she said, startled, waving off the stranger.

Amigo did not move. Instead he stared into her anxious eyes, and then decisively he reached and curled his fingertips into hers, comfortable as carpenter's joint. He touched her so lightly she could not be sure he was doing what she could clearly see him doing.

The music was resonant with steel drums and dueling electric guitars and a big slouch of a man singing, rumblingly.

Amigo drew her to the dance floor. With one hand hovering near her hip, he was not even touching her yet somehow he guided her. His expression was intense. For his part he could feel her body following. He knew exactly what to do with her. Knew precisely how to strum her ignorance.

He had them so they faced each other. Their feet were stepping to the drums, their torsos an inch apart, arms out, palms touching palms, they were clapping against each others hands, the sound was raucous like castanets. She could hardly believe she could keep up with him. He was making this happen, he had led her into this, had made it somehow so she could follow. She was exhilarated and it seemed it was only her and Amigo in the glittering room.

When the music stopped Amigo bowed his head slightly, and turned away. She thought she saw a tattoo of a hand on his shoulder.

AUNT MURIEL

THE TOUR bus was half full and I had a row of seats to myself. Our guide was Mindy from Nebraska. Mindy said that as was apparent from her skin tone, she had only recently arrived. "I've come in from the cold!" she laughed, and hugged herself so that her sunburned breasts surged under a v-neck t-shirt.

We set off from out front of a shell store. Mindy fired up her megaphone and blasted information at her audience. She pointed out Ernest Hemingway's favorite bars, which seemed to include most every bar we passed.

But I could overhear a conversation between the couple directly in front of me. He was obviously younger, somewhere in his twenties. She was somewhere in her forties, with a halo of blonde hair. She stared out the window, which had no glass, so that sounds and smells of town swam around us in hot blasts and stinky surges unctuously, cloyingly. I should have been registering Mindy's description of the court house structure, carved entirely from coral.

"Aunt Muriel," the man whispered, and turned to her. His green eyes were narrowed and portentous.

"I've seen three very pretty girls so far." And he slid one arm across the back of their bench. I watched the arm moving furtively, like a rat snake. It was a youthful arm, with firm biceps of rounded muscles and caramel suntanned skin, and tapering to a square hand and rough blunted fingers. His hand reached the curve of her back. His thumb bounced lightly, falling every so often and resting against the bony ridge of her shoulder blade. The contact was almost imperceptible, like perhaps the jolting of the bus made his hand graze her skin.

When she checked herself in her compact I caught site, in the reflection, of faint lines around gray eyes, and a gorgeous face. He filled up the space beside her with his wide shoulders and a head of wild hair.

Mindy was busy explaining a history of pirates and pink shrimp and sponge divers, only fragments of which I logged. Mindy summarized the caste system of born and bred locals, who call themselves conchs, a symbol of enormous pride, versus the various imports, from the Cubans to the Serbians, the Russians and the Israelis, and of course the disaffected North Americans from their multiplicity of origins. But my attention continually strayed back to the odd couple.

The bus parked out front of the shell store, now closing up. Mindy came around with her ball cap out for tips.

Aunt Muriel was standing up, preparing to vacate the trolley when her nephew, who was already standing, turned to her. Aunt Muriel pressed back against the window, as if perhaps she knew what was about to happen. Sure enough the nephew leaned in on her, crowding her, his face so serious, his long lashed green eyes at half mast. And then he kissed her flush on the mouth.

RAINY SEASON

RECENTLY I bought a bicycle. I bought the bike because I first considered stealing one, but I have no aptitude for crime. Instead, dutifully, I paid for a lime green contraption, with whitewall tires, and a front basket.

I was under the impression that one could not forget how to ride these things, however, I have almost killed myself several times already. It does not help that fearless cats lie out in the middle of the streets. They lie on their sides, heads cocked, and stare at you as you perform wobbly maneuvers around them.

But a bicycle is the best way to get around when the streets flood.

September is the rainy season, and tropical rains are symphonic. In moments, a storm can switch the sky from pristine, to a purple, velvet, padded look. Et puis, the deluge. In an instant, streets are submerged, sidewalks immersed. Whole coconuts bob in gutters turned to rivers, like kids on water-slides.

It is customary in Key West to ride on the sidewalks. I found this spectacularly annoying so long as I was a pedestrian. Now that I am a cyclist I see the merits. Primarily, that one is out of the reach of motorists. However, Key West sidewalks are treacherous. They are irregularly dotted with lampposts, palm trees, and one time, a man sleeping on a low cot. Not to mention, the spectacularly annoying pedestrians. It does not help that these sidewalks, made of concrete slabs, occasionally pitch, like buckteeth, from Jurassic tree roots.

Often there is jungle foliage drooping over the sidewalks, reducing the space to an ever narrowing, green tunnel. Tight enough to crash into, if one was not used to being on a bicycle. I have crashed a couple of times, spiky fronds leave marks like cat's claws.

As quickly as the storms come, they depart. Sunshine infiltrates and rainbows pop out, birds chirrup. The air turns steamy and fills with dense, loamy, flower smells. On my bike I glide through the heavy puddles, and inspect the drenched town. Steam rises. Roosters bark out their mad song. Cats are everywhere, on car roofs, on porch railings. With only the merest curiosity they watch my unsteady approach, on my green bicycle, flicking muddy water, and still they do not even twitch an ear. Cool cats.

STRIP CLUB

IN THE name of journalism I visited the strip clubs.

I went accompanied by my pal Turtle, a local. At one end of Duval Street we swept aside a curtain and entered a low-ceilinged room with a bar running one length and several bodies deep with men dressed in plaid shorts and tank tops and flip-flops, and women wearing nothing at all except for magnificent high heels.

I followed Turtle to the groin of the building, to a cave of a room with dark walls and the center dominated by a platform jutting like a tongue. On this tongue, like so many piercings, were silvery poles and around these poles swung some lithe females. They were naked, except for regulation eight inch Lucite shoes. Turtle blew kisses to the dancers. They smiled and approached.

"They love me here," Turtle declared. My guide knew a notable amount for his tender twenty-something years.

The dancers were young, their bodies gorgeous. Pubic hair was meticulous as bonsai gardens. Breasts were everywhere. The sport with breasts is for a patron to place his face between a pair. The girl will then press her breasts, pinning the face into a mammary sandwich. Turtle repeated this process many times. Once with tits so wide the dancer could scarcely make them meet. Another pair of knockers, attached to a damsel with a velvet choker and gold glitter sprinkled on her pale skin, Turtle claimed, "They have to be fake! It was like I was being punched!"

I declined a turn.

The next establishment was up a rickety flight and inside a clammy low-lit cavern. Here nude girls danced on a stage that snaked all throughout the room. In no club did I witness any stripping, unless you count the stepping out of a thong. Mostly male patrons were seated at eye-level to the stage, their heads tilted, focused on the dazzling flesh. One dancer squatted in front of a customer, firm breasts within milking distance.

Despite the gunmetal glint in her eyes she was fearsomely feminine. Her customer was porcine and grinning fiendishly. His three buddies sat tight, in an excited huddle. She plucked off the guy's glasses and brazenly polished them on her clamshell. Next, she wafted the glasses under the guy's nose. The guy spat up his drink and whooped, his buddies roared. They all tucked paper money into her garter.

My chair was sticky.

A blonde vision swished into view, and Turtle groaned. He nodded at the divinity and she smiled and shimmied over. She crouched down so her pearl farm was in my grille, and said, "Where are you from?"

I blushed when, handing her money, our fingers touched.

She spun away and into Turtle's sights. Gracefully she fell into a backbend, suggesting the entrance to a tunnel of love.

Turtle stared, entranced.

"My greatest fear," he said, "is she is going to fart in my face."

Gold glitter shimmered on his cheeks.

"OUCH!" CRIED Lula Belle, and she raised
fingertips to her head.
"Sorry, Darling, casualty of war," said Charles.

Charles crouched in the sturdy limbs of an orange
tree. Through the dark leaves he could see his wife's
mouth, he watched her tongue licking across her
sunburnt lips. He felt nothing whatsoever as he
watched her rub her temple. "You're the one who
wanted something sweet," said Charles.

The orange tree was in an orchard, on a hill, owned
for generations by the Rodriguez-Lopez family.
Until a few years ago, when the family sold it to the
Englishman, Charles, and his American wife, Lula
Belle.

"I can't believe you interrupted my work, for this!"
said Charles. He squatted, high up in the tree. With
one hand he grasped at a branch, and with his free
hand he reached for the ripe fruit. Lula Belle held
the bucket steady, tight against her torso. There
were three small oranges in it, mottled white and
yellow.

"I don't want oranges," Lula Belle was near crying,
"I want chocolate."
"Hold still," said Charles, and he made as if to lob

35

the fruit. At the last moment he flicked his wrist, giving the missile topspin.

"Hey! Ow!" Lula Belle screamed, and dropped the basket, clutched at her ribs.

Tonio heard the scream. He was walking near the hill that used to belong to his father. The hill where he was born, his ancestors were born, and buried. Tonio grew up believing this land would one day be his. He did not mean to turn his head and look, but he did. He was at the exact spot where he and his brothers, returning home from midnight escapades, would slip through the forest of bamboo, and the grove of lemon and orange trees, from which his mother would make fresh juice. Tonio and his brothers would ease back into hammocks, never waking the snoring family, or snoozing dogs.

Just as when they were children these country boys now grown would leave their homes late at night. Tonio led them to the secret meetings in the jungle. In mud-splattered, threadbare clothes, and scuffed knee-high rubber boots, the brothers climbed the red earth mountain paths, deep into the steep dense hills where no roads would ever be paved. Tonio was a natural leader. One day he would get back his father's land.

Lula Belle gathered up the basket, and the spilled fruit. "I love our life," she said, and instantly, her eyes welled with tears, and she added, under her breath, "I just wish I could spend it with someone other than you."

"Bitch," muttered Charles, as he unwound an orange from its stem, and aimed it at the bridge of his wife's nose, where it exploded.
"Stop!" cried Lula Belle.
"Accident, Luvie, sorry," said Charles, with a thin grin.

What really annoyed her, was that after this pelting, she knew she would be the one to squeeze the damn oranges.

LAST NIGHT I went for my customary midnight stroll down Duval Street, and what did I behold but an impromptu music video organically sprung from out the sidewalk in front of a grocery store slash liquor store slash rolling papers and cigarettes and all type of soft vices kind of store. Like most establishments on Duval Street the store opens directly onto the sidewalk, like an arcade. This store regularly plays techno music extremely loudly.

Along came a gang of youths, none older than teenagers, a couple under the age of ten and quite tiny, well they all began to dance. They were brimming with energy and smiling and pounding out these fast impressive moves to the heartbeat challenging music with its whizzing siren overtones. All of them were jumping and shimmying and clapping with their knees so they looked like gyroscopes. They were rather fantastic and many of us passerby stopped to watch, clogging the curb.

Ambling down the sidewalk from the other side of the street was another group of youths. The newcomers paused and observed the dancing gang, a few were boys still in their teens wearing the shortest of possible red micro shorts with legs so long they seemed to begin under their arms, like flamingos. One flamingo pulled up his shirt and, exposing a torso hard like a two-by-four, rolled the

39

hem into his teeth. Then he said something to his crew and they crossed the street. The dancers saw them coming and ramped up the speed of their gyrations. The flamingos bound and fell right into an energetic dance of their own.

One guy put his hands behind his head, elbows out, and began descending slowly on powerful legs meanwhile motoring his behind so fast it was a blur. Another of the incredibly long legged flamingoes ripped off his hoody and tossed it to the ground and leapt into the splits, falling fast and expertly and gracefully to the cement sidewalk, where he pulsed with pneumatic speed, and then he grabbed himself between the legs, collecting his spilling self, and rolled and tucked, and all the time laughing delightfully. The store's cashiers were also swaying and moving their hips to the music, and clapping their hands above their heads, encouraging the dance-off.

The song ended and the dancers bounced in place, and slapped each other's hands, and backs, and then began to disperse, melding into the thick flow of nocturnal revelers.

And I continued on with my stroll.

DOWNSIZE

CRISP, EARLY November, and Roderick and
Daisy were moving. Roderick did not want to leave
his townhouse. "It's curtains for me. I'm ruined!"
Roderick declared. "The bank owns my toys! Can
you believe?" All on account of some papers he
signed, as he says, "When I was out of my mind!"

Daisy wasn't overjoyed about the enforced move,
especially since she saw it as a backslide to the
boonies. But Roderick was her meal-ticket, and
where he went she was quick to follow. Besides,
Daisy had learned, after a decade as a beautiful
plaything, that when rich people claimed they were
broke it meant something else, entirely.

The new house, a rental down valley, was bare. Not
so much as a knife and fork. Which was Ok since
neither Roderick nor Daisy were big on cooking.
Unless you count holding a flame beneath a
spoonful of junk. Still, even the addled need
somewhere to loll. The night before the move they
went online and ordered furniture. Roderick found a
site with improbably low prices. "Let's get
everything," Roderick suggested, and they were up
all night, shopping and arguing.

Any tension between them evaporated when, with
pride, Roderick watched "Baby", a monster of a
motorcycle, delivered to the new house. One of the

41

few items the bank had overlooked. Largely because he'd forgotten he owned it. Men untied the purple machine from a flatbed, and rolled it down a ramp.

"Baby!" Roderick said, arms outstretched. He hoisted his bulky frame astride the motorcycle. He pressed his soft thighs against the fairings. It felt wonderful. He wanted to feel the wind against his sallow cheeks.

"Back in the saddle!" Roderick punched one hand in the air and whooped, and then he began coughing, hacking, so much he had to grip the handlebars and jam his feet flat on the ground to keep from tipping.

"Lordy!" Daisy said, smacking a hand over her mouth.
"Shhhh!" Roderick whispered. He pushed the key into the keyhole and twisted.

And that was the last anyone could say precisely what happened. There was an explosion; puffs of smoke, licks of fire. The motorcycle thrust forward a few feet, as if possessed, and then wobbled eerily, before tumbling, bits flew off noisily as it met with the gravel of the driveway.

"Owwww!" Roderick was down and curled round like a shrimp; he was hugging his knees, and keening.

The following day, on a stack of pillows and blankets, Roderick was stationed by the living room window. He heard the sounds of a big truck.

"Darling!" Roderick yelled. "Furniture arriving!" Daisy ran down the stairs, two at a time. Excitedly she skipped to the front door, opened it wide. The truck parked, the driver went around to the back and raised a rattling gate. After some rummaging he retrieved a small brown parcel. Right away Daisy knew something was wrong. It was a crushing disappointment to discover they had ordered dollhouse furniture.

HELLO, CAN you hear me? Listen, Michelle called this morning, she wants me to send money.

All I want to do is stuff my face with cake.

Who does that girl think she is? Getting pregnant and expecting the rest of us to look after her.

I am going to the bakery. I'm going to get in my car and drive one hundred and twenty miles, that's sixty miles each way.

Today she tells me she wants me to be the Godfather. Like that's some prize. I don't want to know her baby. I don't want to bond with it.

You know what I want to do? I want to go to the bakery. Listen, when I go I stand around saying I've got five people coming for dinner, so I'll need six of those and six of these, and I really believe they are listening to my lies!

Michelle was crying. She said he beat her up. What does she expect? He's a thug, he's a loser. He's poor. She said she left him and she wants to come live with me! What am I supposed to tell her? What am I supposed to do? How is it my responsibility? If I were a female I would not be getting knocked up by anyone poor. No how!All I want to do is eat cake.

She said he stole her jewelry. She has nothing. He even took her clothes. She said she's in rags. Can you imagine.

By the way, after the bakery I make another stop. KFC. For a bucket, and dippin' sauce. Yum-Eee.

Michelle needs to go ask one of her wealthy relatives. I can't help her. I can't have a baby in my house. Next thing the impregnator will track her down and move in here, and kill me, and kill my cat. I shan't take her call when she phones...

My routine is first I go to the bakery. Next I get me my KFC and dippin' sauce. Next I go to the car wash. And in the car wash, when the car is all soaped up and sudsy, and no one can see me, and I'm finally all alone, I devour it all. I stuff the food into my face in an orgy of out of control piggery. I feast switching from sweet to savory; I jam it all into my fat face.

I feel so guilty...

I'm going to the bakery. I'll call you later.

SNAKES ON A PLANE

WHEN THE Arab lady walked onto the plane I was not the only one to notice. In a long blue dress with a blue sheer wrap that went over her head she was hard to miss. Another Arab, a man, strode onto the plane. He was unsmiling, with dark hollowed out eyes, and stiff black hair. A hush descended when yet another swarthy man, younger, entered the cabin. I was buckling my seatbelt but I kept one eye cocked. Husband, wife and son, I hoped, rather than suicide squad. When the lady in blue and the two men started down the aisle passengers all around noticeably swiveled, audible as wind riffling autumn leaves, as most of us couldn't help ourselves from staring at the profiled personages.

The plane took off and our fate was sealed. Screens descended from the ceiling and a movie flicked on, distracting and lulling us. Until, that is, the pilot crackled through the speakers.

"Howdy folks, can I have your attention please, nothing to be concerned about, we're gonna make an unscheduled stop. Gonna let some folks off."

The aircraft dipped and swooped to the right, tracking west. Faces swished around, eyes darting as we caught each others worried looks. No doubt about it I felt the thrum of panic.

Flight crew emerged, ostentatiously calm. "Everything's fine," they murmured, patting headrests as they passed, "Nothing to worry about." This had the exact opposite effect with everyone suddenly twitching.

The captain was back at the intercom, "Sorry about this, the new plan is we're going back to the original plan, we're heading for our original destination. Sorry for any confusion. When we land I'm going to ask you all to remain seated until the police have removed someone. Thank you for your cooperation."

The movie was all but forgotten now passengers were whispering loudly, practically hissing. Many of us were flashing knowing looks in the direction of the Arabs. I could barely see them but they looked guilty to me, they were staring at the floor and keeping quiet.

Until the landing gears were engaged, the wings flicking their little extra flaps, the flight crew strapped into their jump seats, the atmosphere was charged.

"Folks, please remain seated," the captain oozed over the PA, as the plane bumped and noisily slowed down the runway.
The cabin door opened and we all craned. Chilly air scented with gasoline preceded a team of gun-toting uniformed police hustling aboard.

"Are you the lady who was causing trouble?" The lead policeman said. Except, oddly, he was not addressing the blue-frocked Arab lady. He was speaking to a diminutive caucasian female.

"I don't care," the girl said, and began to sob. After some back and forth the police were escorting the tiny, sobbing figure away. Befuddled relief permeated as we learned she had, allegedly, picked a fight with a passenger in first class.

I forgot about the Arabs in the commotion to exit.

EVAN & ELLE

ELLE WORRIED about him, he had twenty years
on her and he was getting on. She wanted for his
dreams to come true.

At seventy Evan acknowledged this was the home
stretch. It was unbelievable to him, but it was a fact.
He was officially old. He had been good to Elle.
Had put her on a pedestal. If she were to tell the
truth she would say she was never 'madly in love'.
But she appreciated him. Mostly for the passionate
way he adored her.

If you knew him you knew this was merely his way.
He was passionate about whatever he did. He had a
wild side, but he exercised discipline. All his life he
had done the right thing. They were introduced
through friends when both were widows. She was
looking for a fresh start and he was needy for
company. They met and married while he was still
employed. He was a pilot, having learned the craft
during his stint in the military.

"Evan is hot in his uniform." Elle liked to say.

From the onset they felt they'd known each forever.
They were comfortable together. And she liked
having his big old house to herself during the days.

Elle loved to cook. All day long she cooked and sipped her wine.

Evan didn't like it when she got drunk. She could get a little reckless with the commentary. But he never complained, because it was not in his nature. He refused to waste a moment on negativity. Evan always said after he retired he would prefer to live somewhere warm. His whole life he had lived in a cold climate. "Don't get me wrong, I love it here, this is home!" he'd say, one hand massaging a shoulder, "But I don't want to die of a heart attack shoveling snow!"

After he retired she found him in her way. He loved her cooking, and in his enthusiasm he always made a mess in the kitchen. Sometimes, if he left a dirty plate on the counter, instead of in the sink, she lost her temper. It ruined things for her, his being home, underfoot. She started to feel differently toward the house. She decided she had never really liked it.

"Let's move to Florida." Elle proposed to Evan, one evening over dinner.

The way he heard it, she was doing this for him. To make the remainder of his life as full as it could be. He cherished her for her selflessness. They divested themselves of the house, and its contents, and purchased a purple hippy van, with tiny curtains on the side bubble windows. To Evan this was pure paradise.

They wended south, until the weather began to improve. As they crossed the State line into Florida the sun came out. They were smiling at each other, confident they had made the right decision.

From nowhere came a truck, smashing into them and their purple van.

FOR ANYBODY interested Evan and Elle did not perish in the automobile accident. While their van was demolished to fragments, they walked away unmarked, physically.

As for psychologically, they were enhanced, if anything they marveled at life all the more. The experience had filled them with renewed verve, for a bit. They were somewhere in northern Florida and it took Evan and Elle a few days to sort themselves out, putting up at a worn motel while shopping for a car.

Soon they were on the road again, now kitted out in an old tub of a station wagon, chocolate brown. The only thing evidently wrong was a tricky light bulb in the dash, and it was priced to sell. They were headed for Key West, "Because life is wonderful but life is short," as Evan said.

Elle, in the front passenger seat, made a game of lowering the visor, sliding wide a cover which in turn switched on a light over an embedded mirror. Elle tugged on her lower lip, and jutted her jaw. Evan thought this made her look like a fish. "What are you doing?" Evan asked, less patiently each time.

"I'm looking for gold, my darling," Elle responded, staring at the watery pink reflection of her gaping mouth in the mirror. Her critical eye zeroed in on the seemingly trillions of lines around her lips and her thoughts soured.

Late in the day and the chocolate brown tub motored south of Miami. Here the daylight waned and stars flickered on. A smile of a half moon leered in the darkening royal blue sky. The highway narrowed and road signs abandoned all pretense of prim civility and blazed colorfully lit billboards of pirates and naked ladies and lots and lots of liquor stores.

"Sips?" Elle whispered, in her infantilized way. Instead, Evan sunk his foot on the accelerator; half convinced that if they could just reach their destination everything would be ok. He tried to distract his wife with anecdotes, junk he had memorized earlier that day, back at the rank motel. This worked for a few miles.

"I need vino!" Elle implored suddenly, starting to cry softly.

With a couple of hours yet to go Evan felt outgunned and he pulled into the welcoming bosom of a 24 hour drive-thru alcohol warehouse. When he rejoined the highway Evan was concerned to notice the dashboard lights were dimming. He was having a hard time making out the controls. But with the

glow of Key West visible he decided to go for it.
After the best of a bottle of merlot Elle was
defanged and the couple merrily accompanied the
Rolling Stones on the radio, singing heartily, "I
can't get no…"

From nowhere came a truck, smashing into the
station wagon…

,

AT 2AM I was walking down one end of Duval Street, heading for my car, headed home. I walked accompanied by the usual night-symphony of revelers raving and ambulance sirens and rooster calls, when I heard a ruckus.

A group of three crocked spring-breakers were stopped and gesticulating and cursing loudly at a doorway. I posted up by a wall, and observed. The trio caterwauled until finally out of steam they staggered off. From the entranceway emanated peeling guffaws. Gingerly I approached to investigate, and in the doorway I found two men on the front stoop of a small hotel.

One guy, salt & pepper beard and beetroot skin, was seated protectively in front of a box of beer, he was chortling, and pointing at his friend. His friend was reclining flat on his back with his legs out stiffly in front like he was levitating. He had his hands folded over his orange teeshirt and he was spluttering, maybe even choking a bit, wheezing and rocking with laughter. When he sat up I saw his red face was streaming with tears. It was a face stuck all over with joy. Pure and infectious, and I asked if I might sit with them.

Al and Nick are a couple of Maryland lads in town
for Nick's 40th birthday. They traveled with their
spouses and their motorbikes. Their last night in
paradise, with the wives tucked in bed upstairs at
the hotel, the men rigged a game with a toy fishing
pole, a yellow plastic thing they bought for three
dollars at the corner drug store.

Nick sported a crew cut and flame tattoos on his
forearms, "They match my bike," he explained, "I
was having a midlife crisis." Nick let out his line
and sent his buddy Al to place the lure on the
sidewalk, a dollar stuck with quarters, as sinkers.

The passing drunks were pitiably hilarious as they
lunged at the money. Nick skillfully wound the reel,
hauling in the bill as the sot snatched, with face
contorting from confusion as the dollar flittered
from a grasp. After each catch Nick slumped
exploding with giggles. Al too, eyes closed,
cracking up. Their elation transformed them and I
saw them as carefree kids, before the pile up of life.
Both Nick and Al were slung with shiny green
party-beads. Nick's game was luminously innocent,
yet temporarily triumphing in this prurient town.

Eyes bugged as the dollar flew away. The
bewilderment they expressed was priceless.
Impaired minds followed the skittering bill before
registering us, and our hysterical faces, momentarily
sobering them, like a slap. "Fuckers!" decried an
intoxicated girl, her high heels dangling from one

hand. Later she returned and said, "I called you 'fuckers'. I'm sorry."

We watched a montage of stumblebum fishing all set to the melodic cacophonic track of our cruel laughter. At daybreak they packed up their equipment and we split the memories.

AFTERNOON

I BICYCLED against the wind, pedaling slowly to the end of a pier of flagstone.

I passed a small boy on roller blades, maybe ten years old, he was wispy as a stalk with a thatch of yellow hair shading a serious face. With a hand against a rock wall he shoved off, skating straight and steady. All was fine until one wheel snagged and he lurched and came apart. His legs whirled, boots jackknifing, desperately he had his arms spinning. I held my breath. It was going to hurt to land on that unforgiving flagstone. All of the little boy juddered and it looked like for sure he was going down when a whisker away from impact he softened into a noodle, righting himself back and up, balancing himself. I never saw him blink.

Sun dappled behind fast moving clouds while all along the beach people had stopped in knots to watch a determined beginner on a kite-board. Frequently there are kite-boarders flipping on the waves and bounding in the air, spraying water like diamond beads against azure skies, but I have never seen a novice, never witnessed the humbling struggle. He appeared young but his body was soft, with meringue-white skin and narrow arms suggesting a life spent thus far mostly indoors, today he was standing in the ocean up to his pasty waist. He was focused on a flap of fabric in the sky, and wrangling with the cords connecting him to the kite jerking in and out of currents. He stood wrestling with his rigging with his instructor nearby, dressed in half a wetsuit, relaxed against the heaving waves and calling out encouraging plays.

Seagulls and pelicans swooned around the kite-boarder and his bobbing instructor, occasionally hurtling fast like arrows, spearing the surface, plucking at the silver fish that move around in balloons of metallic shimmer, sometimes leaping as one out of the water, through the air, creating ridiculously pretty tiny blizzards. Someone was grilling and the tantalizing smell of roasting meat traveled like a salesman in the breeze.Suddenly the sky darkened with whipped up clouds and noisy winds scattering dry leaves, and I was surrounded by skateboarders and bicyclists and mopeds. Wind spun sand squalls. Groggy-eyed sunbathers made for their cars, laden and shuffling on slippery flip-flops. A man was running in a strange scuttling way, with his back hunched. Then I saw in his arms lay a sleeping child and he carried her with one hand holding her head.

And the rain came down, gigantic drops crash landed noisily. The raindrops were warm like bathwater and they felt wonderful.

JUMBLE

I WANT to die! Can you hear me? I have to tell you what happened to me, before I commit suicide.

Joe Boy thought it would be hilarious to send me his collection of dirty old porn videos. I spread them all over my bed to take a look. It was that porn from the 70s, those cheap looking videos of men with pimples and hair. You know, they were very hairy back then. They were just shocking. And I'm thinking what am I going to do with all of this? I don't want to watch it. I don't even get horny. Those days are over. Don't get me wrong, if my lover ever gets out of jail, well Ooo la-la! Otherwise I am a solitary man. And I don't care. I have my movies, my soufflés and my cat. Isn't that right Mr Fat? Silly fat cat!

Do you know we had a snow storm? This morning my car wouldn't start so I phoned the specialists to come take it away on a flatbed truck. You know how it is with German engineering, I can't simply hand it over to just anyone, I have to get the most expensive most experienced people around. It's going to cost a fortune. I'll have to beg mummy to help with the bill. Ok, so my doorbell is broken and I had to leave the front door open, you know, because I might not hear the mechanics, and they will just leave and they will never come back today. You have to remember I'm in the boonies.

So the front door was open and in flew this adorable tiny owlet, practically right into my arms. Then it went crashing against the ceiling and then up to the second floor, and it was bumping into everything and crying. Oh, I felt so bad for the little guy. Poor creature! I know how to handle birds because I'm a trained expert, I'm certified, but he was just a baby and I don't have owlet formula on hand so I called the lupine man, I mean the avian man, the bird guy, whatever, anyway I got a hold of him and he said he'd be right over.

Picture this, the car guys are hoisting the Benz, and the bird guy and I are on the landing, sort of outside my bedroom, when, oh my God, who would have thought ninety-four year old Mrs Richards would climb the stairs in the first place? And I couldn't even throw myself on the bed to cover up the videos because I was holding the owlet!

Mrs Richards said she wanted something for the church jumble. And everyone was staring at the porn! And it's not even my taste!

Oh my God! I want to die! I'm so humiliated! I don't know what to do with myself. I need a drink! I'm going to drink cognac and watch my favorite movies and then I'll kill myself.

TEAMWORK

THEY WERE a wretched sight, mother and son, hunkered on yellow plastic chairs at the police station. They sat at the lip of their seats, suggesting free will, meanwhile they huddled, stiff and frightened looking. The way they positioned their limbs obscured the handcuffs and lengths of chain tethering them to one another and the metal desk. The young man fussed with the locks, worming a toothpick into the hole, while mom blew him a kiss and winked.

For decades these low-rent schemers had mustered a living from genteel crime. Mom would conceptualize and son would implement, tipping cars off cliffs, staging robberies, faking injuries. Only one time did things get out of hand when setting a house ablaze they accidentally charred half the neighbor's. "Hey!" the mom assured, "No one got hurt."

The father was gone long ago, his car crammed with everything they ever owned, never to be seen again. The son, from an early age devised a mode of his own. While craven, he was a nimble-fingered thief and instinctively he knew this was a talent he ought to develop. In candy stores he cleared whole shelves, silently stuffing his pockets before moseying off. Eventually the mother discovered her son's penchant, finding him and his pilfered candy in the basement.

"What's this?" she said, hands on hips, as her son cowered and immediately confessed. "Who is my good boy!" she exclaimed, and gave her child a smothering hug.

Entwined as they were by their proclivities, they teamed up. When the schemes worked they took their winnings and shoved them into burlap sacks and buried the loot in a bog.

"Crime does pay!" the mother extolled.

Their favorite activity was acquiring. They exhausted themselves with purchasing. They were gluttons and they gorged, wiping the sweat from their brows with soggy paper money. It was a while before they noticed the karmic strings attached. For one thing, the money had to be stashed in a filthy freezing cold hole. Getting at it was trying. Time passed and they got sloppy, no longer bothering to look around and check who might observe them pulling bags from out the arsehole of a field in the middle of effing nowhere.

Mom was returning to the car, the fourth such trip that morning, dragging the dirty bag of cash, letting it jounce off slimy clods. Bills fluttered loose, gone on a gust.

"Mom! The bag!"

"What?"

"The bag! It's spilling!"

The sack had split its seams. Tattered white fringe bust in all directions, while bills swirled, twirling on the cold metallic breeze.

It was bad luck a trooper was passing by. Of course he saw enough to warrant a look-see. Mother and son were transported to county jail where they sat in the yellow plastic chairs, whispering, and fussing with the locks of their restraints.

TANDEM

FEBRUARY IN the tropics and it is balmy. The nightly party that is downtown Key West is swept clean early everyday. Streets freshly watered, like hair slicked for chapel, and all visible trace of the night before is erased. But nothing can contain the smells rising like an insistent mist, mingling with the warming day. Other than a longhaired skateboarder lashed to a galloping multicolored dog, Duval Street was deserted when I went for coffee.

At the corner of Caroline Street I saw them. She was folded on the handlebars of his bicycle, she faced him, unsmiling. His arms were stiff arcs enveloping her as he steered the black cruiser. He was moving fast, and beaming, and she looked utterly relaxed, with an eery unnatural calm. He zipped from sidewalk to street, slinking around clumps of awakening pedestrians gathering out front of cafes sipping from lidded paper cups. Quite out of place in the steamy Keys he wore a dark wool suit, riding with his knees out wide, his black lace-up shoes like arrows on the pedals.

She was in a dress of gray netting, spiky and see-through, her skin was pale, her eyes languorous, long kinky fair hair framed a serene face. She was a mermaid caught in her fisherman's net.

She was glorious, yet oddly glum, meanwhile her beau grinned. Their faces were close. They were not talking. Occasionally his head jutted forward and he kissed her. Their private world drew stares, and he nimbly maneuvered, at quite a clip, passing by bemused onlookers craning to take in the engrossed twosome.

They might have been pedaling to their own wedding, as likely as being on their way home from a long night. There was something about their intensity, the cliche tableau. And then Elvis rode past on his scooter, today in his cherry red and sequin jumpsuit with lapels like fins. Tourists held up flashing cell phones, and the bicyclists were forgotten.

I would have clean forgotten about them too, but later that day I saw him again, riding his same black bicycle down Duval Street, now abuzz with cars cruising, and taxicabs. He no longer wore the dark wool suit but it was unmistakably him, for one thing he had on those shiny black leather lace ups, city shoes, memorable footwear in a beach town. He looked ecstatic, just as earlier when I had espied him, and sure enough he was not alone. Filling in the space between himself and the handlebars was a person. A female. Sort of folded, same as before.

Yet something was different. I tried to get a decent glimpse without being too obvious. People thronged and I could only catch snippets. Something, however, was off. Gradually I realized she was not the same girl. This one a brunette. They kissed like lovers, until she caught me gaping, slack-jawed. The last thing I saw before reluctantly turning away was the picture of her joyous face.

I won't tell.

FLORA & FAUNA

LIKE A sword with its hilt exposed and blade in the
earth, I found a rusty machete. Inspired by the
flower-scented day I decided I should try
horticulture. I marched around my garden cutting
everything unattractive. To tidy up some ragged
browning tips I chopped at a plant taller than myself
with impossibly long leaves like gigantic rabbit
ears. Horribly, the stumps proceeded to leak sticky
beads of milk with a garish stink like molten rubber.
I had hurt the thing. I felt awful and I began to
apologize, but I did not know how to convey my
sentiments. Should I hug it?

I continued hacking away at some seemingly loose
palm tree bits but they were more robust than they
appeared and the blade ricocheted on each slice and
I pictured losing an eye, or fingers. When the
machete came close to cutting off one entire arm I
lanced it back at the leaf strewn ground.

To remove myself from danger I pitched into the
hammock.

I have seen cats cutting through the back yard.
Singly they stride, favoring particular routes. A
calico male insists on spraying a low shrub, which
does indeed sport a lustrous patina I had previously
put down to good health. To be neighborly I nightly

75

placed a heaped plate. Every morning the dish was spotless. This continued until I discovered the plate rimmed with small brown snails, their slimy bodies like squishy tongues suctioning away. I'm told gargantuan toads are often found face down in the cat food.

One night I saw a black cat sitting stiffly in a patch of shade. Unseen, through a window, I stared. I made out the strip of white chest and one white paw. Gradually I realized the cat had no face. Where its face should be instead there was nothing, only shadows. Squinting, I stared harder and all outlines dispersed. I blinked and the cat vanished, dissolved into varying depths of darkness, fuzzy blackness filling the space between giant green leaves with serrated edges. The white chest turned into the edge of a flagstone, the white paw a leaf.

Another night a pair of raccoons trotted across the top of the back fence. These tropical raccoons are smaller than their northern brethren. One sprung to the ground in a graceful leap and attacked my yoga mat. With his jaws he ripped free a mouthful. And then the little furry beast shook his wrinkling snout, and spat out the unappetizing fragments before scrabbling up a tree trunk and racing away to rejoin his comrade. A corner of the mat is forever gone, tiny teeth marks outline the crime scene and I no longer leave the mat out at night.

Easing off the hammock I went indoors for a glass of water, and on my way I checked up on the slasher-victim fern. The globules of oleaginous cream were caking; hopefully I have not murdered flora, or poisoned fauna, nor perturbed the ghost cats.

OPHELIA WAS titillated about the gig, almost as much for the chance to get out of town. "I need me a good time," she said to herself as she packed her favorite ruby red dress.

Meanwhile, Isaac and his father were sailing in the Gulf of Mexico. As was their habit, weather permitting, they blew fare-thee-well kisses to long-suffering Mom and the Outer Banks of North Carolina and sailed south.

Late Saturday afternoon Ophelia convened with her band mates at the luggage carousel in the Key West airport. First thing she said was she was off to get her hair and nails done. She sent the band ahead to set up at the saloon. Toto, her faithful drummer, loves Ophelia dearly, but he is the first to admit, "Ophelia can be quite the diva!"

Isaac and his father whiled the day snorkeling, spearing fish and trapping lobsters. On one dive, Isaac reached the reef and gradually focused his eyes to see an almighty dorsal fin. "First thing I did was freak out," Isaac shook his head at the memory. "I pissed my pants and that made me freak out even more coz I heard somewhere sharks like the smell of piss! I was out of the water and in the boat before I figured it was probably a nurse shark."

Between sets Toto stole some calm in an alley, lounging against a wall, his sneakers gluing to the beer-sticky street, he sucked his cigarette. "Ophelia calls me and she's like, 'We gotta gig!'" Toto laughed, checking over his shoulder he added, "What a diva! We never even rehearsed! She's like, 'Just play!' We are making all sorts of mistakes!"

Isaac and his father anchored near the main marina and grilled their catch, and invited neighboring seafarers. An odd-job assortment joined, trading in alcohol for the wondrous feast. Afterward Isaac excused himself. "Dang!" he thought, stumbling toward town, "I gotta do the Duval crawl at least once." As was his way, when he was soused, when he came upon a good-looking lady he would glide up and murmur, "You are so sexy!" Generally the female reacted by going rigid and bolting. "I'm straight coz that's my test!" he explains, "If she can't handle that, she can't handle me."

Inside the club the air was dense with sweat, liquor and smoke, and Ophelia was singing her heart out, beguiling the audience with her smile, lassoing them with her voice. The crowd was dancing and melting sweating.

Isaac paused in the entranceway. Instantly he was rapt by the passionate blues, and his blurred vision crystallized at the sight of sumptuous Ophelia and her ruby red dress. He waited until he caught her attention, then he mouthed, "You are so sexy!"

Ophelia never missed a beat while she sang and swayed and stared at the sassy young man. With eyelashes the breadth of butterfly wings, she winked at him.

HOME

LAST NOVEMBER I signed a lease on a plain bungalow with an appealing garden. I pictured genteel gatherings of my new cultured acquaintances, sipping chilled drinks and snacking on delectables I would concoct; I could learn how. Gradually I had to admit I will not be hosting any natty parties with homemade anything. For one thing, my place is usually a mess. Naturally I tidy up once a month before the maid comes, because I'm embarrassed for her to see how I live.

Giving up on the garden party hallucination I have allowed piles of things to grow unchecked. When I first inspected this domicile it looked lovely. For all sorts of reasons (mostly revolving around my utter lack of patience) I was dashing around in a big hurry and I failed to notice the bedroom lacked a window, like a cave. I discovered this long after signing the lease, so I decided to learn to love the cave.

Nightly, reluctantly, I lay down in the cave, and steamed away like a sticky pudding. I'm an insomniac/hypochondriac/claustrophobic with a vivid imagination, and my dread of being buried alive was now revisited on a nightly basis. I tried to learn to love the cave, but I could not.

Last night I cracked. Gasping at tiny breaths of hot fan-stirred air lying sweating in the cave, I could take no more. I sat up and flicked on the lights. I leapt out from bed and kicked the mattress until it sloughed from the box spring. Slowly I heaved it into the living room and leaned it against a wall. Next I hauled in the box spring and shoved it into a corner. Of course the mattress smacked me in the face as I positioned it in front of the box spring. A tap and it wobbled over and into place.

I reclined on my unmade bed, now in the living room, and became entranced with the lofty beamed ceiling and the walls of windows and the soft life-giving breezes that wafted across my skin. It was spiritual and I loved it. I slept with angels. I awoke to find my head under the desk and my feet in the kitchen. My little home was in shambles. I wished I had done this months ago.

The kettle was whistling when the phone started ringing.

"Hello?" I said groggily and poured the boiling water over a teabag and into my cup.

It was a gentleman, "I'm making a documentary of Key West authors," he said. "I'd like to include you."

I sat on the edge of the bed and carefully blew on the hot tea. "Go on." I said.

"So far I've met with…" and the man listed the local luminaries. The man continued, "I'd like to film you at home."

"Right," I said, and I sipped my tea and looked around, assessing the chaos. "May I call you back?"

THE DANCER

IT WAS a Saturday night and Duval Street was busy. Half way along and something was causing a bottleneck; a throng was stopped and blocking the sidewalk. Even the street was choked with slowed pedicabs, with drivers craning, and they have seen it all. I had to see. I elbowed my way through to find at the center of the circle of the commotion was a single small girl dancing inside a hula hoop. But by dancing I mean mesmerically.

The little hula dancer had some moves, seemingly creating a tunnel around herself, supple as ribbon as she trained the hoop from the end of one finger, and pulsating the fast moving hoop all the way down to near her ankles and with a bend to her knees she had it traveling north again. Hips moving in a continuous O.

Seated close by, and wholly ignored, was a skinny shirtless man on a type of horn that he held with both hands but its stem carried on longer than his whole body and resting on the dirty cement sidewalk it pitched up at the end in a cornucopia of haunting sounds.

Her hair was multicolored and twisted into wide dreadlocks, pulled back into a stiff ponytail. Her clothes were tropical gypsy replete with a sheer scarf sewn with a hundred golden coins, so that they shook and sparkled like electric plumage. She was so sexy she emptied the mind and filled the heart. As she danced her face remained serene like a confident child.

She played up to the passing motorbikes and they nearly toppled. She out-performed herself for the big trucks and the windows rolled down and admirers hung out. Grown men yearned to take her home, make her whole. She nearly caused traffic accidents.

When she did these moves her guy on the horn followed her with his eyes meanwhile his mouth stayed stuck on his instrument. His music was sublime and the little hula girl had evidently danced to it a trillion times, they shared a tangible communication and even with her attention diverted he could reel her back, so that they were moving together, like a snake charmer and his happy pet.

Repeatedly I dropped money in their tip jar, an upturned top hat. I could not walk away; rather I did not want to.

Occasionally obscuring my view were posses of brides and their maids, and then groups of grooms with their stags, usually someone carrying a naked blow-up doll, and most everyone smoking the local hand-rolled Cuban seed cigars. Men and women and some well trained pets puffed the cigars. The sweet heavy smoke mixed in with the hot still air and car fumes. The unctuous smell took me back as scents have the power to do, to a time long ago, sparking memories of when children were encouraged to believe in dreams and fairy tales, like the adventures of the dancing gypsy girl.

AWAKENING ME too early was knocking at the
front door, accompanied by squeaky voices calling,
"Hello, hello?"

Pulling my somnambulant self together I discovered
a brace of boys on my stoop. The children were
dressed like accountants.
"Yes?" I inquired through the latched screen door.
Pinned to breast pockets were nameplates printed
with Elder Ebenezer and Elder Jeremiah. At most
they were twelve years old.

All glossy-eyed Elder Jeremiah piped up with, "We
want to pray to Jesus with you!"

"Go to hell!" I said, which I thought was pretty
funny. Unfortunately the boys did not and,
perplexed, they backed away whispering anxiously.
When I boiled water for tea I chuckled, I should
have netted them and slipped them into a cauldron.

Regret slowly crystalized as I envisaged inflamed
relatives of one or both of these runts paying me a
visit, upbraiding me. I should have been nice to the
little blighters, I rued. Reservation for one in Hell,
please.

Meanwhile a pal asked me to check out a band, friends of hers. "They're a trio from Boston and they're awesome!" my pal said. "I'll tell them to expect you."

Strolling to the venue I was overtaken by some exceptional drumming and I stopped to absorb the syncopations pulsing from an open-fronted bar. In the back a smoky room, on a platform stage was a band of a dozen men on percussion instruments. The sound was bracing and I wanted to dive into its lusciousness, except I had an obligation. And onward I went to the tourist-centric plastic venue with twenty foot mugs of beer dangling from the rafters.

I settled at the bar, and prepared to love the lissome trio performing. My ebullience dissipated as I determined the trio were not awesome. And I couldn't walk out of the club because there was just me and one doublewide denim clad family, with bulging sunburned skin. To be polite I stayed to the end, to say hello, as per my pal's instructions.

Eventually the caterwauling stopped and I went and gushed how genius they were, because truly I was so grateful they were done. I strained to make conversation but my efforts fell flat and we remained awkward. I offered up my hilarious encounter with the Godly children at my doorstep. Blank stares, not so much as a titter.

Later, when I Googled the trio I learned they call themselves a Christian band. Good Lord, I'm going to hell.

I bid adieu and spirited back whence I heard the exceptional drumming. Miraculously they were still going strong, the vibrations of their song palpable and irresistible, I merged into the dancing crowd.

A girl bumped my hip with hers. She wore an emerald green fringe-edged dress and bare feet. Leaning in close so that I had to inhale her musk, she said, "If I lead, can you follow?"

"I can try!" I said, and I accepted her hand.

ON SUNNY days geckos bask on the back steps, positioned at the corners of the stairs with their prehistoric snouts raised in salutation to the sun. Geckos are very small and pose no threat, but their skittery movements unnerve me. Initially I hated them, I tried to spook them to scare them off, I would rush at them, arms out and waggling and making frightening noises, but they merely stared at me as if perhaps I needed help. Over time we developed a truce.

All was well in my animal kingdom until one day, as I peaceably daydreamed at my computer; absentmindedly sipping from ice water with key lime juice when a flash caught my attention. Snapping me from my woolgathering I saw a baby gecko peering out from behind a stack on my desk.

He was tiny and translucently pale, and it appeared he was smiling the smile of a supplicant, like he was imploring me to help. Of course I wanted to help, plus I wanted him out of the house, the thought of him springing over me as I slept gave me the creeps.

Remembering how my friend Nalim had tackled the innocent owlet of some weeks past, I dashed for a towel. The miniature reptile stayed crouched beside the stack, those trusting eyes staring at me. Tossing the towel I pictured great mariners loosening seines and hauling in catch. Picking up an edge I peaked beneath to find nothing. No baby gecko. I shook out the towel but he was gone, never to be seen again.

Perhaps I befriended some of these geckos, but it was hard to be sure, plus it seemed I never saw the same beast twice. One afternoon the birds began chirping hotly so I skipped to a window to see and was affronted with the dreadful sight of an oily length of blackness slithering through the grass. I didn't trust my eyes until the grotesque spectacle recurred. Now a walk in the garden is fraught, every rustling steeped with possibilities of the monster looping up a limb and garroting a major artery, or fanging me with venom.

Today I was surprised to see a tidy pile of dog poo, black and shiny and pretzeled beneath a green and wicker garden chair stationed beside the back steps. Then, shockingly, from the top of the slimy heap I saw an inky flickering tongue shoot out. The crafty snake was hiding from view of the suntanning lizards, my friends.

Were I a naturalist I would have coolly observed, instead I freaked out. All of me quivering I slammed closed the rattling screen door. Geckos bound away in all directions and Mr. Snake oozed into the grass, diminishing to a tip that remained upright, like a middle finger.

I wonder if I should drag the hammock indoors, line it up alongside the bed in the living room? As my friend Nalim said, "Even Eden has its snake so you must be in Paradise!"

I JUST got home from the Doral Resort, in Miami. The hotel complex was bigger than Key West.

I was visiting for the weekend with friends competing in the Judo Open. My friends, who flew from New York, are former champion and legendary columnist Taki, coach and practitioner Teimoc, writer and Judo black belt Mark Brennan, and Brian Pereira, the only one of the troupe competing. Brian is the youngest and the newest to the group, and the best looking.

Friday I accompanied my pod to the auditorium where the Judo US Olympic trials were carrying on, on a couple of enormous yellow mats, surrounded by five chairs deep in spectators. The room was generally near capacity with a lot of traipsing to and fro of competitors, coaches, news-camera operators, parents of competitors, and audience. Chances are good I was the only one in there who had never before seen Judo and knew nothing about it.

Watching that first match, Friday, what struck me was how I knew absolutely zero about Judo. To me, Taekwondo, Karate, Jujitsu, Aikido, Judo well they were all that Asian dude slicing through the air and taking down enemies with some chop-chopping with the hands, and back-flipping kick routines.

I continue to know nothing of the nuances of the other disciplines but what I will say for Judo is it is sensational to watch. What looks like a person falling turns into an exact position like a praying mantis, stiff and yet twitteringly poised for movement, defensive or offensive. The athletes are awesome to observe.

I watched a match between a lanky Swede and a gorgeous Argentine, who eventually dominated the tall perfectly formed Swede. The Swede was mighty pissed but under control. I had seen the Swede earlier, in the hotel lobby, with his girlfriend and an old guy, Taki said the old guy was the coach. The match was two men grabbing at each other's lapels, and sometimes sliding out a foot to topple the opponent. Sometimes this worked and they both crashed to the mat, but instead of hitting the floor feet flicker or legs fly and the two continue to move. It's a very awesome dance and I was gripped. Taki narrated, telling me the names of the moves, which sounded like Chinese menu items.

Next a couple of ladies, an American who was fierce and tense and a Cubana with a beautiful face and a sneer for a personality. The Cubana demolished the American, but as slowly and impassively as metal corroding to a pile of dust. All the women I saw spent a lot of time fixing their ponytails. La Cubana's coach is a man so corpulent he leans back so the front of him is leveraged like a prow. Even his oily stringy black hair is sliding off

100

the back of his head, tumbling into a snake pit of wet curls at his collar, around which hangs his credentials and a silver whistle on a rope.

Next some boys, a Russian and a Cuban. The Cuban dominated, but it was grueling. They were even, too even, the Russian was sleek like a bullet, like something designed to withstand endless beatings, and he did. The two were panting at the end. The ref told them both off for wasting time, performing a tumbling move with his arms to exhibit his displeasure, but it seemed to me the boys were not prevaricating so much as they were whipped, they were catching their breaths. Big cats with stomach muscles like I've only seen in pictures. They beat they pounded they dragged each other around by the lapels; they stared at each other in utter concentration. Then they might suddenly flip or very quickly move, I could not always make out what was happening, it was mostly too quick.

And sometimes they slam-land their opponent flat on his/her back, making an almighty noise, a thunderous crack, sounding painful. At the end, after the Cuban won, he could not speak, and to answer questions he would smile or shrug or point at things and all the while panting furiously as he made his way out of the exhibition room.

Dinner was steak and grog and fun on open air South Beach, and over early to accommodate Brian. He might be assigned the first match of the day at nine am. He and Teimoc would be getting up early to warm him up.

Saturday morning I got a good seat before start time. I watched eight hours of Judo. I loved it. Sometimes matches are over in a trice and you ache for the defeated and their occasional illegal displays of anguish. The movements, the foot work is all so impressive, so fast and so precise. "It might look like they are falling, but they are not," said Taki.

Brian had four matches, one was a default in his favor, one he won and two he lost. One of those losses was to the Swede, who did not win a slot on the Olympic team, but went on to win the Open.

Saturday night we ate more steaks and drank more grog. Brian finds it less terrifying to go up against a Judo black belt than to approach a female. After fortifying himself sufficiently he asked a pretty girl to dance.

CARD SOUND ROAD

THE MIAMI hotel was surrounded by meticulous golf courses dotted with dramatic fountains. Everywhere were well tended shiny green shrubs with swells of florid flowers. Crows cawed evilly, otherwise the noises were of the cars swishing around the circular driveway where valet-parkers formula-oned at perilous speeds.

Walking from one hotel structure to the next I met with wafts of cigarette smoke, like streaks of dirt stuck in the humid air. Sunday, when it was time to leave, I could have dawdled and taken advantage of the spa facilities, had a massage, been pampered. Instead I set the navigation thingy and pointed the car southbound. Obeying the instructions I thanked the bitch for each suggestion, and reclined my seat like a gangster, and settled in for the long ride home.

Any other time, any other place, I generally get seized by the need to travel as fast as possible, even though I know full well this means I will arrive at my destination feeling horrible. I've never questioned this urge, only ever given in to it, like some demented homing pigeon. Soon the madness of Miami and a thousand lanes of racing machines dwindled to one lane where the speed limit is 35mph, which is almost impossible unless you have a clear visible view of the police.

And then I saw the sign, 'Exit left for Card Sound Road'. I'd heard of this road and I was tempted. So instead of my usual tunnel vision, I flipped the turn signal and was promptly delivered into a scruffy forest.

The forest remained dense and there wasn't much to see and I wondered if I'd made the right decision. Suddenly on either side of the road were a cluster of shops, all fish themed. This short busy stretch was a town comprised of maybe five shops and a lot of pickup trucks with fishing poles like rooster tails. Then a toll booth, one dollar and I was heading up a bridge so steep it could have been at an amusement park. Thin humped bridges from which families fish, and all around is an endless spread of blues and greens of glittering ocean, under sultry multicolored skies and huge slow moving birds and far away puffy pink clouds. All so beautiful, making it impossible to want to hurry.

The road is a ribbon of white satin bumpily connecting uninhabited islands of tangles of mangroves, so that one is bounding over shimmering aqua in what feels like zero gravity giant strides on a world of water. It was an incredible treat. Eventually the road ended and rejoined the main highway connecting the Keys.

Home in Key West I am all the more appreciative of the glamorous natural beauty, of the sounds of the cheerful calypso of birds, of the robust smells of flowers and sweet soft air, and the jubilant crowing of the roosters. I'm back in Paradise, which reminds me, now I must attend to that snake.

ON THE FLY

FIRST I would like to thank those of you who offered suggestions for my sabbatical month. I liked the suggestions so much I have decided to do them all.

As I was loading the car, I pictured driving around America. I could stop at the fishing villages along the Florida coast, later maybe also fly to New York. I was slamming the trunk when my phone rang. It was a local girl offering an empty guest room across town. I sped right over. She was in the middle of trying to eradicate an infestation of white flies. An entire gumbo limbo tree was turned snowy from fly issue.

"You can stay a couple of nights," she said.

I stayed a week.

I used up the week watching my hostess try a variety of homespun white fly killing techniques, the best of which was the purchase of five thousand ladybugs. Too soon the week ended, and at the last moment I bought a ticket for New York. En route to the airport I drove the ocean road. I had a few minutes to spare so I parked at the beach. I made my way to the edge of the gentlest of surfs, water too placid to make headway up the sand. I reveled in the bright seascape and the warm air and tried to absorb the loveliness. Hoped to freeze the scene in my imagination.

"That you?" The words broke up my trance. I already knew the voice, I turned to see a friend from town. We have never learned each others names. He is my favorite dance partner at the Salsa club.

"Hello!"

We embraced. "Wassa matter your face?" He said. "Why you look so sad?"

Magician-like he fired up a marijuana cigarette and stuffed it twixt my lips. I did inhale. Then I inhaled some more. We giggled, and slumped on the confectioner's sugar sand. We listened to the collision of bird calls. We watched the diving gulls and pelicans, precision bombing the water, flapping back up toward the open sky with tiny, black, squirmy fish clamped in their beaks. Swallowing on the fly.

"Flying!" I jumped up, and patted my friend on his head. "Gotta go."

Turned out I was tremendously stoned, and it was a Herculean task to park at the airport in what seemed a very tiny narrow spot. And then to haul my bag, which suddenly felt like a thousand pounds, to the terminal. In my mind I heard the eerie synthesized soundtrack to Midnight Express. I trembled, sweat started rolling hotly down my spine, tickling the small of my back. Once aboard, I passed out before takeoff.

It has been a week since I got to New York. Right away it was good to be back. I have dashed hither and kissed cheeks yon. I have been busy as a butterfly. And I cannot help wondering if those five thousand ladybugs are the start of upsetting the ecosystem.

I CRASHED a fancy book party in a private home on Park Avenue. I was not much interested in the author, or her book, or even the free comestibles. Truth is I had heard of this domicile, and I was curious. The owner, Oliver, is a rich man, a businessman, respectable. He is known as a philanthropist. He is older, he is serious, he has a splendid home, people frequently remark on it, "Get yourself invited to one of Oliver's parties," people will recommend. But they don't know the half of it.

I was watching Oliver as he entertained a coterie. All slightly stooped, and bobbing, like they were bowing. Their drinks glasses held out in front of themselves, like begging bowls. I watched Oliver. He was paying close attention to a sleek lady talking at him. Without much of a plan I strode toward him. I gained on him, and then I was standing next to him. He continued nodding enthusiastically at the woman. She went banging on. I moved closer to Oliver, so I was right up on him. I leaned in close to his ear.

"I know everything about you," I half whispered. "I know Vera Voluptus."

Oliver spun like a well oiled ball bearing. He gripped me at the elbow, and steered me away.

"What news of Vera?" He spoke staring at the persian carpet. Vera was one of those girls who can hook a man for life. Vera claimed to be South American. She looked the part, with a lot of glossy black very long wavy movie-star hair. Gossips liked to say she was a liar, and she was really SheenaLynn Wiener, from Weekawken. Since we live in a results oriented atmosphere I say it does not much matter the provenance. Her results were good. She had some very pale skin, and a passion for party outfits. Vera always looked divine, even after a week of cocaine. Word was her makeup was tattooed. Vera was book smart, and stunning. She could ski bumps, could serve an ace, was disciplined about maintaining "the outline" as she called it.

The first time I met Vera was in a bathroom. There she was, bent over the sink, her face close to the mirror, applying makeup. In between sniffing from a tiny brown bottle. "I like you," she said. "But my mother always told me never trust girls."

One time at a party Vera quietly asked me to spot her twenty dollars, for a taxi home. I upped the money, never gave it much thought. Until hours later, Vera long gone, somehow the topic cropped up. Apparently Vera had asked everyone of us in the room for twenty bucks to get home. We could only laugh, reluctantly impressed.

From the start I wondered what happens to girls like Vera.

Way back then Vera would tell stories about Oliver and his Park Avenue house. Despite his baggy oatmeal colored corduroys and his shapeless navy cashmere crew neck with the merest hint of a stiff white collar peaking over I knew that the nebbishy philanthropist was a wild drug and sex animal.

"I heard she's living with her crack dealer," I whispered to Oliver. He stared at the floor. He shoved a hand into his corduroy pocket, produced a business card, and thrust it at me. "Call me," he commanded. And then Oliver took a few steps and returned to his gaggle.

I CHEWED up a fortnight in New York at a friend's apartment on the thirty-sixth floor overlooking Central Park. In two weeks I almost never left the building, except sometimes very late at night, for parties.

Carlos, my host, travels constantly, for his work. He has a spacious home he is never in, and a car he never uses stashed at a garage.

A housekeeper and a couple other house guests came and went, but I was mostly left to myself. Delivery men materialized at the front door, all day long, bearing foods, and clean clothes, and whatever else.

Carlos and I have a frayed history of friendship that was tight, in its heyday. Unfortunately, we met with a falling-out a couple of years ago, and have not spoken much since. This was an opportunity to reacquaint.

And I might have stayed longer than two weeks except a guest room opened up in a large house in Westchester, and I bolted. To facilitate the move I borrowed Carlos' car. In true sociopath fashion I justified my actions, with "I need it," and "Carlos will never know."

Seeing as I did not ask permission, technically I suppose you could say I stole it. Obviously, I had no intentions of keeping the machine, not forever. But a few days passed while I wallowed in Westchester, with the car in the driveway.

Early in the morning on my third day Carlos phoned. I saw his name on the caller ID. It was far too early for good news so I knew I was in trouble. I ignored the call and went back to sleep. No need to deal with being scolded any sooner than absolutely necessary.

Later, after a shot of whiskey-spiked coffee, for pluck, I returned the auto. Carlos was mightily rightfully pissed.

On the train back to the suburbs, I left old Carlos a message, I said, "Seeing as I was considerate enough to bring back your car, you could at least come visit."

Carlos has not returned the call.

THREE DOG NIGHT

I'M STAYING with my friend Mabel, in Westchester. Mabel runs a battleship of a home-front, with innumerable offspring, and a village in staff, not to mention assorted pets, one of which was a week overdue with four heartbeats detected. The expectant mother was a caramel-colored long haired low-rider wiener with old eyes. The father a tiny white puffball that was partial to yapping incessantly. Despite itself the excitable beast was endearing. Even after he left his still moist gnawed T-bone stuffed in between my pillows.

By my second day two of the four children had been dashed to the ER for various conditions, bee sting allergies and the like. I managed to elude too much direct interaction by submerging myself in a lot of very hot baths, or borrowing one of the many cars in the driveway and poking around the neighborhood.

To slot oneself in with a bustling household is an experience. For one thing all the noises are related in some way, unlike a discordant city. Even the yipping tiny dog was more percussion than annoying. I found I liked lounging on the blue chaise in my room, in the terry bathrobe hung in my bathroom, and listening to the sounds of this home.

On my third day I said to my hostess, "I usually spend all my time by myself. But I'm liking this 'being with people' thing."

Mabel frowned at me. "This is your idea of being with people?" Mabel asked. Her dark eyebrows raised, her black eyes glistened and flashed, like trains rattling away into mountain tunnels. "Sitting in your room with your door closed? That's your idea of being with people?"

We stared at each other. Mabel crossed her arms, and pursed her mouth. "Watch out, bad weather is coming," she warned, and she turned and left, already dialing on her cell phone.

The bad weather was a freak blizzard, dumping a couple of feet of snow in a matter of hours. It managed to turn off the power for half the county. Friends and neighbors moved in, seeking warmth, until Mabel's house also lost power. Not to be defeated Mabel bust out years' worth of camping gear. A brazier and fire was lit, cocoa was miraculously produced bubbling hot.

The many children made games of the snow.

Night encroached and we decamped to nearby hotels. Last thing before abandoning the battleship was to lock up the white dog in Mabel's bathroom, with bowls of food and water and chews and toys.

"Behave, you hear? You've caused enough trouble already," I scolded the energetic powderpuff, meanwhile stroking his impossibly soft fur.

Mabel's youngest, ten year old Joshua, admonished me, "It's not trouble. It's a blessing. New life." I have a lot to learn.

Even though the hotel rules were 'no animals permitted', thankfully Mabel had thought to smuggle in the wiener where the little dog promptly gave birth. One loss, one breech, three new lives. Hallelujah.

120

END OF AN ERA

I'M IN 'the city' and coincidentally today was the
service of a friend. I decided to attend.

Turns out nobody knew he was ill.

Until just the other day, when news got out that he
was not well, and then the next thing anyone heard,
he was dead.

Now here we all were, in the middle of the day,
sitting in a Greek Orthodox church on the upper
east side.

I had no idea he was Greek.

I did not know him exceptionally well. Even though
our acquaintanceship spanned thirty years. This
man was the lover of a friend of mine. He was also
my mother's gardener. Together they created an
Eden of gardenias and mint and basil in gorgeous
pots on her terrace, penthouse, midtown. To another
he was a fellow acting student with whom to spar in
the lead roles of Death of a Salesman. This man,
now deceased, was many things to many people.
But by all he was much liked, in a word, he was
irreproachable.

Everybody in the church knew him at least as long as I, most longer.

The eulogy was delivered too low, and not a word of the lovingly crafted composition was heard.

The last time I saw him was at a Halloween party, a year ago. I sat with him at a round table in a fantastically decorated room. We talked about my mother's garden, and how sad it was that she sold up and moved away. We both loved that pretty terrace. When she left, 'It was the end of an era', we agreed. I was glad to see him.

The biggest celebrity at the service was Bolt of Lighting, that was her name, or something like it. She looked no more than a very stylish sixties, but everyone whispered she was at least eighty. She had a raccoon coif and all swept up into a fat ess shape. Her mod-outfit was also black and white, and her black, very high-heeled shoes had red insteps, like tongues.

Bolt of Lightning was the first in line to go view the open casket.

I have heard of this habit, seen renditions on the television and in the flicks. But never personally in the embalmed flesh. The two to my left, friends, indicated they wished to join the line of mourners.

Thus, I felt compelled and trudged with them down the aisle.

I had the inclination to swoop my eyes around, check out the church and gather in the crowd, but I did not dare, especially after I noticed a friend in a front pew was crying. His face only ever before seen laughing, jettisoning pith and wit, today was set with sadness, eyes wet with tears.

The open casket was a sight to see, a first for me. The nose looked so much more pointy than I remembered. The skin was an unsettling muddy purple. A Halloween mask. I could not stop from flinching. Amen, friend.

THANK YOU

ALONG WITH most everyone in Key West late in the afternoon I watch the sunset. Dazzled by the beauty I chase a primitive urge to honor the event. The gold disc that is the sun hits the horizon and throws down what looks like a glistening path of mercury spilling on the ocean surface, scattering right to my feet.

After the daylight fades and the temperature drops and commingles with hints of jasmine, I push off, counting on the wellspring of belief that after the darkness and the frights of the night there will once again be a new strong life-giving sun. Walking from the beach, saying goodbye to the day as much as hello to the night and the popping stars, I remember noticing the claw-tipped paw prints of dogs in the sand.

In some Slavic countries Christmas is called Bozhich, which means little god. While clearly this cleaves to the Christian concept of Christmas, the name is likely of pagan origin. The myth revolved around worship of the birth of a young, new god of the sun replacing the old, weakened solar deity on the night of December 22nd, the winter solstice, the longest night of the year.Like members of a cult we revere light, endowing it with supernatural hope. We perform rituals of light-worship for the new day, New Year, new life.

Firecrackers for every day of the week. Forms of encouragement to help endure the dark, as we lumber toward the nourishing brightness.

A bartender with a twisted hemp ponytail told me he believes he has witnessed the local Serbian population, "Very late at night," he said, taking a long pull on his filterless cigarette, "They turn into werewolves."

"They transmogrify!" He said, and whistled out blue smoke. "Watch out!" He said. "You'll only catch a glimpse! Like the end of a tail going around a corner!" I almost believed him. And then he said, "With my own two eyes, like, I've seen them, heard them, in the woods, carrying on."

Around this time of year the Keys are washed by cataclysmic storms, noisy and powerful and short, almost frightening although soon supplanted with a dripping sticky musk air, aromatic as a bakery. But last night, amid the thunder and lightning, I distinctly heard howling, and I shivered.

We distort shapes from shadows and hear our name in the wind. In the murk we are inclined to see what is not. And in the shade we double up any illumination, using bounce, like a face lit by a candle flame.

While writing can often feel like grappling in the dark my motivation is the radiant bounce reflecting from the satisfaction of the reader and thereby brightening the life of the writer. Bounce, in this case, is thank you. Thank you for making the writing so very enjoyable.

The pleasure is entirely due to you reading it. Thank you for your time. I wish all of you the merriest of partying, pagan or otherwise.

HAPPY NEW YEAR

THE DAY began with an iguana falling out of a tree. That's how they get around. They simply permit themselves to sag from a high perch. The bright green rubbery beast landed heavily on the hammock, gripping at the rope contraption with his too long clattering claws. He saw me, a beat behind my following his antics. He froze and anticipated his certain doom.

Technically he was dead. He was mine. Except I had no intentions whatsoever on murder. I merely observed. He took his time before eventually hauling himself over one side. He lunged onto a leaf the size of a suitcase and from there he slithered into the thick shrubbery that marks the edge of the garden. I got the feeling the iguana had taken this hammock route before and I determined to cast an eye about next time I settled in for a kip.

To offset total sloth I went for a bike ride. With the sun in my eyes at an intersection I slowly put together the pixels of the busy image ahead.

A rumbling gathering of mopeds, each ridden by someone bronzed, toned, in little more than shorts and sunglasses. I stepped down from my bicycle, and leaned against it. I had reggae on the headphones and it was wonderful to watch this spontaneous parade, ebullient as butterflies. And as they passed they tipped their heads, a nod, each with a smile, and to each I nodded in return. By the time the last moped chuffed away I was outright grinning.

Later, near the beach, lights blazed. By the water's edge, in between some palms, a man was detonating fireworks. I perched on a lava boulder, and inhaled warm briny air entwined with sulphur. Silver flares emitted slivers in a bristly shower, first shooting straight up, noisy as a train's whistle, level with the top curving fronds of the trees and there the rockets exploded with their final burst, silvery fire shaking free in all directions.

Circling homeward I gazed upon a couple of lovers strolling arm-in-arm. She was cherubic and alluring with a baby-girl pouting mouth and long russet curls. In blue jeans shorts and cowboy boots she was adorable. Her fellow was loping alongside her and they were deep in conversation, with their heads lowered, in their own world, as they made their way beneath the shade of trees.

Shaggy hair obscured his face but I thought I recognized him. I think he's a Serb, he pedals a pedicab. I realized I've never seen him ambulatory. His walk is particular, somehow fluid, rolling smooth as hydraulics. They turned at the corner, dragging a shadow.

Suddenly, like a shotgun blast I recalled what the bartender told me about the werewolves, and how at most you could expect to see a tail vanishing around a corner.

Should I warn the lass? More likely she was long ago bitten and is beyond salvation. Lucky lady.

Happy New Year!

NIDIFICATION

I AM moving again, this time from one side of Key West t'other. The rental I have occupied since spring has been rented, to others, and I must move, immediately. For the millionth time in my life I fill my car with my gear. A friend will take me in for a few nights. But I waste no time and with the help of online listings I am on the case finding new digs. This being a tiny island, I swiftly visited a pile up of unlivable quarters, unless, of course, one was routinely inebriated, blind and insensate. Early this morning I saw a fresh post on the electronic billboard, it read, 'hidden gem'. Anywhere else I would have had my heckles up, and brimmed with suspicions. But here, where people say 'good-day' when they pass by in the street, I knew that 'hidden gem' was going to be the real thing. I made an appointment to visit.

In this town rentals go fast, the nice and the not nice. One day you may see a red and white 'for rent' sign hanging off a white picket fence, and the next day you will see a moving van and a person, grinning, carrying in their possessions.

Who knows if down the line some unforeseen horror will rear and ruin my life. I've been fooled many times before and that includes two ex-husbands (another story altogether). But I fell in love with the 'hidden gem', before entering it. It was a carnal lust that wrapped me up and I signed a year lease before my future landlord had time to run my references. I employed my most convincing English accent (acquired after years of otherwise useless education). I thrust my books on the man, by way of introduction.

The hidden gem is concealed by a very plain house that sits on the street, under a streetlamp. To the side of the plain house there is a lacy wrought iron gate which opens to a path. This path plunges directly into a sculpted jungle of banyans with Spanish moss, and here sits the gem. A treasure of a house with French doors opening up to the garden of banana trees and orchids, and a fountain, sounding like a brook. Butterflies and dragonflies buzzed the shallow pool. I signed the lease on the spot. It was only after the ink had dried I thought to ask about the furniture (there will be none), and the move-in date (November 1st).

Now there is October to fill. What shall I do with myself while I wait for my abode? I could get in the car and drive around America, and have adventures. I could go to New Orleans, a destination that beckons. Or return to New York City for yet another last hurrah. It would be an expedition couched in the coddling embrace of ego-puffrage, and book parties.

As they say in Key West, "What would Papa do?"

I SCREAM, AGAIN

MY LANDLADY scheduled a visit. After four
months we had never met in person. Chillingly, her
child got muddled into our plan. I decided on
opening with something terrorizing so as to keep the
brat at bay. I had a presentiment of horrendous
damage. But I had a list of things that needed
attention.

First thing the kid did was crawl into my hammock,
half slipping and grappling, like a drunken bug in a
web. Thankfully her mother admonished her, "No,
peanut!" and yanked her to terra firma.

I presented the list. My landlady is a stunning
blonde with periwinkle eyes and there's nothing she
cannot fix. We went to some monolithic hardware
store that she was intimately familiar with. The kid
sat cross-legged in the wheelie cart. The other
shoppers were predominantly men, quietly grazing
in their zoned out way, until she swished by and
they could not help themselves but crane.

Back at the ranch mama moved rocks and coral
boulders and was up to her elbows in mosquito
swamp effortlessly fixing fountain pumps and
replacing rubber hoses and plastic parts. In high
heels and a long dress she installed screen doors and

fixed air conditioners and rewired a fan. I was in love.

Meanwhile the kid and I began to play. Despite her pink dress and ribbons she was a tomboy. Soon, mud was churned and clung in her hair and smudged on her face. I decided I liked her. Being half feral myself I was moved by the urge to share my toys. I scooped the tiny girl into my arms and placed her gently on the hammock. Before I lay the child down, I whispered, "If you need to move around you have to move very slowly. Ok?" She assured me she understood the drill.

I promptly forgot about her and got busy marveling at mom's dexterity. I was petitioning her, asking if she could maybe stay and look after me, when suddenly we heard piercing shrieking.

We turned to see the hammock flipping, and the child flying at the ground with her mouth wide with terror. She was grabbing at the warping canvas, except it was flapping, and she could gain no purchase. The inevitable crash was made worse when her delicate face smashed directly against the wood supports. The only thing louder than the noise of impact was the screaming.

I had to cover my ears.

The mother cradled her child, muffling the pitiful howls, absorbing the pain. Patting fast-rolling tears on the traumatized baby-face.

Thank heavens no skin was punctured, no blood was shed. Really, it was nothing more than a protruding tomato-red welt on her forehead. A disfiguring bump that we all pretended was not nearly as bad as it looked. Surely it would go down?

The weeping dwindled to moans.
"Mom, can I have an ice cream as big as the world?"
"Yes, peanut."

I suppose they won't be visiting again anytime soon.

NOVAK DJOKOVIC

DEAR NOVAK,

I have started a breeding colony of super talented
hot Serbians and I need your DNA- just kidding!

Seriously, you are the number one tennis player in
the world; and you are number one in my eyes.

In Miami you played a tough game against Marcos
Bahgdatis. You both played magnificently and it
was not an easy win. So, personally, I don't think
cheering your own victory is at all arrogant, as some
critics purport. When you had Bahgdatis down and
rolling around he reminded me of a barely alive
iguana, when the tail is still swinging around but the
spinal cord is undoubtedly crushed. For Bahgdatis,
just like roadkill, death was collateral damage, not
murder.

With the eyes of the world on you, after defeating
the Cypriot, you signed the lens of a camera thrust
in your face. Just like your hero Pete Sampras, you
are mentally strong.

You are a winner and you are marvelous to watch.
You are a natural ambassador for Serbs, a people
who could use some light shone their way. After the
war sponsors weren't interested in a young Serb.

Attitudes and times change, as inexorably as the globe rotates, and in large part due to Serbs like you.

I am born in New York City, and thus American but I too am a Serb, at least half. What does it mean to be a Serb? I question nature versus nurture in my quest to better understand. Perhaps these days to be a Serb is to be misunderstood, to be prejudged. Like most Americans I'm constantly on the hunt trying to figure myself out. New studies suggest nature has the greater influence over nurture, which means it's in the genes, and you need to know where you come from to discover who you are.

According to William Wright's superb book Born That Way (Knopf), sense of humor and competitiveness are inherent, and beyond mere family there exist shared cultural traits. Djokovic loves to do funny impressions, I too am a goofball. He loves to throw rackets, so do I, as did my sister Catherine all throughout our childhood. Privileged to be introduced to the beguiling game of tennis when we were teenagers, we rebelled; stubbornness is also, allegedly, a Serbian characteristic. Many a graphite racket was reshaped, like tree tops in the wind, by hurling them at the fence surrounding the court, where sometimes they stuck. After countless hours logged in front of a ball machine I discovered I was not much enthralled with working up a sweat and retreated indoors to watch televised matches and sip iced lemonade and write stories.

Well done Novak, I wish you all the best. After conquering tennis if you want to be a footballer, or a singer or an actor I will follow your journey with keen interest.

Your number one fan,

Christina Oxenberg aka Kristina Oksenberg

Ps: shout out to Princess Jelisaveta Karageorgevic, and Ana Ivanovic, and all good Serbs.

*PEACOCK*S

IT WAS not entirely his fault, but the man was an arrogant bastard, everyone said so. John was the eldest child of a wealthy family. He was raised in a pink marble palace on land which had been in the family for centuries. The house was surrounded on three sides with sloping lawns. A family of pigmy albino peacocks ambled freely, crowing.

By the age of ten all John knew of life was being dragged away from various pleasures to be presented to his parents. In velvet suits, John and his siblings were made to stand, in order of height, at the foot of the grand staircase for their parents to inspect them. This was often terrifying as Papa was explosive, especially late in the day, before he had his wine.

John was his mother's favorite. He got away with the highest of crimes with her. Instead of punishments she fawned over him, stroked his blonde curls, and softly said, "I won't let your father find out." To this day John will tell you he blames his mother for teaching him how to lie. "That bitch!" he liked to say, "She showed me woman is weak when faced with man." In time he would be beastly to his wives, and his mistresses.

John was born handsome which made his mother adore him more and his father care for him less. In hopes of gaining his father's approval John pursued a career as an athlete. He represented his hometown in the national sporting competition. Several years in a row, while in his twenties, he placed second in the high jump and the javelin, winning silver plates with his name engraved.

John would bloat with pride and rush to show his father the trophies, and each time his glee was demolished when his father would scowl, and growl, "If you were a girl I could understand!" Before grabbing the prizes, and sneeringly examining them as if they were soiled undergarments,

"Men take gold!" and with a flick of the wrist he would slice them over the balcony, where he took his afternoon constitution, and watch them plant, like setting suns, into the grass. Once, by accident one supposes, a trophy struck a peacock, took its head right off. Father and son stared as the headless body, with full plumage spread, slumped, twitching. The head bumped along the lawn, rolling like a snowball, with the trophy spinning alongside. Amazingly, the head stopped on the upturned silver plate, as if ready to be served.

His parents died in the fire; along with half his siblings and some of the staff. The structure survived unmolested by the terrible flames that had otherwise liquefied the contents. Rumors persisted that John had commissioned the tragedy. Some teeth were found in the ashes, little more.

In the afternoons John took his tea and cakes and wine on the marble balcony, as his father had.

OFF MY ROCKER

CRAZINESS IS a festering concern for me and periodically I doubt my sanity. I have tried to devise algorithms by which to measure my madness, if indeed there is any. So it was a given I'd check out Jon Ronson's new book. Ronson, of The Men Who Stare At Goats, brings us The Psychopath Test. I perused it with interest.

Out on the balcony of my second floor apartment I tipped back and forth in the wicker rocking chair, working a rut into the floorboards. Ever since relocating to Key West I've developed yet another tic, worshipfully watching the sunset. In between chapters I glanced up, espied the dissolving day and inhaled the sensual feast in the enveloping richness. Is this crazy?

Interrupting my research Joon phoned with a proposition. Joon lives in Hoboken, in a shiny new apartment with views of Manhattan. She sent Jpgs. Her home is airy and bright. There's a full service saloon in each of the supersonic elevators. Well, I exaggerate, but you get the flavor. I said yes a shade before Joon asked me if I'd like to rent one of the many bedrooms. Deluxe, super comfortable and I'd only have to contribute a pittance. Best of all I would get to live with Joon, a friend I adore. Caught in the incoming tide of excitement, I said yes.

Drifting from reality I imagined life with Joon, saw
a mental montage missing only a soundtrack. Us
sitting on a sofa, sharing a laugh. Us in the kitchen,
me on a countertop, Joon chopping something leafy.
And then I saw her leaving for work in the
mornings and me burrowing deeper into bed,
blackout curtains drawn, snuffling like a truffle pig
beneath layers in a chilled cave. I saw eons
potentially sopped up by hibernation. I saw how
eventually I would have to leave the sumptuous
apartment. I would have to go outside and meld
with the crowded planet that is Hoboken.

I pictured the traffic and I thought I could smell the
metallic air. Summers of cement-refracted heat,
winters of dirty snow. And then a rooster crowed
his throaty long call and I looked around at the
green palm trees and the pink and white Victorian
houses. Checked up at the bruising sky and the glow
from the receding sun that brightly hemmed the
edges of clouds shaped like sails.

The Psychopath Test serves up some scientific
research though weighs in more heavily with
personal observations. It is great entertainment. It
posits if you find yourself asking if you are a
psychopath, the answer is no. A true psychopath
does not question themselves.

I think a better test is ask yourself, if you were
living in Paradise, would you move to New Jersey,
even for the deal of the century?

From the rocker on my balcony gazing on a riotous sunset I phoned Joon, "I love you dearly, and thanks all the same, but I'm not psycho."

MOSQUITO SEASON

THE LOCALS had warned of this. With shame stricken faces, they had ominously said, "it can get bad." They told of how the rainy season would incite the mosquito population to engage in wildings, when the insects tear across the island, stabbing and sucking on the red-blooded. Well, it's half way through the Mosquito Season, and I have yet to be bitten.

My houseguest is of Haitian extraction. As a welcoming gift I bought him a book. This book came with a small blue doll and a set of pins, portable Voodoo. I left it out on the kitchen counter, where I knew he would see it. Sure enough, his first evening he picked it up and examined it at close range, and I watched his expression change from calm to cloudy. With a flick he let the little book drop to the counter, where it bounced once, and flounced to the floor. The Haitian wiped his fingertips on his shirt front, and then he yelped, and slapped at his neck.

"What's the matter?" I had to ask.

"Something is biting me," he said, and he spun a tight pirouette, and smacked himself in the face.

His first day he woke up horribly ill, all my plans for the adventures we would have, were dashed. Instead of swimming with the dolphins, the Haitian was holed up in the guest room with paper tissues in his nose.

Our first evening I talked the Haitian out of the guest room and into joining me for a gaze at the stars in the garden. In no time, mosquitos showed up like bikers to a rally, overexcited and raring to go. Amusingly, it turned out the insects only went for the Haitian. His ankles were torn up, while I remained unmolested. Sneezing and scratching he abandoned me and returned to the sanctity of the guest room.

On his second and last day the Haitian rented a scooter and agreed to permit me to sit behind. I learned it is not good scooter etiquette to swivel dramatically as I craned about, "Oh look!" I'd yell into his ear. "No!" he would reply. "Stop moving around back there." Also, I learned the importance of hanging the hell on. As, after waiting on traffic lights to change color, I would tend to space out, and release my grip, and then the bike would go forward, my neck snapping to catch up.

A girl on a moped with flowers stenciled all over, passed us, and stupidly I felt compelled to point this out. Immediately, the Haitian leaned forward, elbows out, shoulders flush with the handlebars, and sped the bike up as fast as it would go. I closed my eyes, and inhaled on the sweet smell of exhaust fumes. Without the benefit of sight the mopeds sounded like mosquitos. When I heard the engine rev down, I opened my eyes. We were caught up with the girl on the flower bike. Sod bicycles, I'm buying a scooter.

AUTHORS NIGHT

AUGUST, AT a friend's house for the weekend in Water Mill. I came to participate in the East Hampton Library fund raiser.

What I love about the Hamptons is the sound of the crickets at night, hearing the whistle of the train in the distance, the smells of cut lawn and sweet flower-scented air.

The library event was spectacular. Bigger than ever, the tent was bulging. I had planned to walk around and meet the authors but that never happened. I was selling books and chatting with people. And soon, of course, I got competitive and needed to sell more books than the authors seated on either side of me.

To my right was a gaunt man with a book about an accident, human error, lives were lost, yawn. Along for the ride was his wife, obviously the eater in the family, who insisted on wedging her way in between us, which was impossible so I had to growl at her.

To restore her equilibrium she tore into plate after plate of boiled shrimp which was pretty disgusting. To my left an angelic lady with a book about an art theft told from the point of view of a dog.

I figured I would probably win my secret competition. Besides, I was armed. I did this event last year so I knew to come prepared. I had extra books to foist on anyone with the least bit of clout who could advance my career (or improve my mood). I had business cards and spread them in a tidy fan on my bit of table. Most importantly I brought a cut crystal bowl that I filled with tiny silver wrapped chocolates.

I was going to get people to visit my bit of table one way or the other. "Chocolate or literature?" I asked those sauntering by.

My pile of books began to dwindle. I carnival barked and even resorted to imploring. "How about if I flat-out beg you to buy my book?" I went so far as to offer a money back guarantee, "If my book does not make you laugh," I assured, "I will send you a refund." My pile whittled down a little more.

Also there was the enormously popular Dick Cavett (his wife bought my book), Martin Amis (I sycophantically forced my book on him). "I have a present for you," I said. "Thank you," he said, unafraid, unsurprised, the famous soft pink boyish face rumpling into the tiniest smile and then shyness got the better of me and I dashed away into the thicket of the crowd.

There were plenty of well-known writers, from Michael Connelly, to Nelson DeMille, and Shere

Hite in full Kabuki makeup, and on the list went from the heavyweights all the way to myself and the dog book lady who I liked a lot.

After quite a bit of arm wrestling I sold off my pile of books.

I already can hardly wait to do it again next year.

DRUG DAY AFTERNOON

Cole is a drug dealer in present day New York City. I chauffeured him one afternoon.

He settled himself in my car and was careful to buckle his seat belt, recommending I do the same, "That's why the cops will pull you over, something simple like a seatbelt."

Cole is fiftyish and grey and rumpled and a shopping cart away from looking homeless. He wears a messenger bag with the strap across his chest like a pageant sash. He says he is an alcoholic though not so much into drugs because he finds them boring. "Boss used to give me free weed, for personal use, but he stopped when he found out I was selling it."

Our journey began on the Upper East Side; our first destination was 50th Street and 2nd Avenue. Cole had an appointment with a 20-something Wall Street guy with a cocaine addiction. Cole never made a comment on my driving, but I noticed he curled, shrimp-like, against the passenger door.

"I got into this business because I don't need a green card a resume or people skills, and there's always work. This trade is unaffected by the economy. The only time we get hit is if we have bad shit for too many weeks in a row. We do get complaints and we offer a full refund.

"Policy is if you don't like it, give it back. I've heard it all -it made my nose bleed, it gave me a headache, it made me nauseous. And you did it all? Then you don't get a refund." Cole heaved forward and spasmed like he was going to throw up. Then I realized he was laughing. At his stop Cole got out of the car and made his delivery while I idled beside a green awning.

"Times Square, Jeeves." Cole instructed. "You're only seeing the mundane side of my job -the traveling around town. Usually I'm in the back of a cab. I pass the time observing humanity. I observe but I stay mum. You can't say anything to anyone here."

We were stopped at a red light and Cole stared at the jostling throng all around us. I saw a look of sadness in his eyes, at the lost potential of this bounty of humanity.

"One time when a pretty girl walked by I did 'yum yum yum' noises at her, and she turned and looked like she was thinking about phoning the police. I said, 'oh I'm sorry, I didn't know 'yum yum yum' means 'fat and ugly' in your language.'" For a second time Cole lunged forward and issued a rattling hacking laugh.

The closer we got to Times Square the more acutely I noticed police, in couplets, on motorbikes or horses, lounging on cement bollards. The police were everywhere. I felt increasingly twitchy and uncomfortable as it sank in I was aiding and abetting.

I started to sweat as all I could see was me cuffed to an interrogation table in a basement cell at The Toombs being tortured into divulging my sources. In my mind's eye I could see myself serving up private contact information on everyone I've ever met. I'm pretty sure I'd crack in less than 30 seconds. I became distracted and almost ran over a pedestrian.

Cole's phone buzzed. "Yes. Hello Martin, Hi-Tek? Not today. Tomorrow. Sorry Mate. Call me tomorrow." Cole shut his phone. "Focking moron."

"Safety measures include you never take a train or a bus. The greatest hazard of my job is my boss, John. He's a smart guy but he smokes too much and he's losing his shit. For one thing he likes for me to meet him in restaurants. Not suspicious at all, walking into a restaurant and sitting down with him, no thanks I'll just chew on a breadstick. I hand him a stack of cash and in return he gives me a bulging plastic bag, not a bit suspicious. One time I was leaving the restaurant when a waiter tapped me on the elbow.

I looked down to see I'd dropped a trail of baggies of marijuana. 'Pick those up, no one has noticed yet, pick them up and get out of here.'"

Cole got out of my car at 47th Street and Broadway and asked me to drive around until he phoned. He had a point as there were militias of blue uniforms on street corners. "I hate midtown. Sometimes I want to tell the customer, why don't we just meet in jail?"

I felt mildly guilty as I privately acknowledged I'm easily the greater danger to Cole than any of his clients.

"I'm uncomfortable when I go to someone's home for the first time. So I figure the customer must be uncomfortable too. Why wouldn't they be? They'll say, 'do you know Tony?' and I say yes, and I see that makes them feel better. But I'm already in their home. I'm thinking 'what if I said, No, I don't know Tony, and now I want you to give me all your valuables.'"

Cole's phone went off. "Karen, hello. You home? 20 minutes?" Cole snapped the phone closed.

"My second day on the job I answered a call– some guy in the Village. I got to the building and it looked okay, doorman and everything. I rode the elevator, and as I got to the front door of the apartment, before I even knocked, it swung open. In I went directly into a fancy hall. Through an open door I could see a huge naked bald man playing with himself and staring at a television screen. I did a double-take, but sure enough he's watching a porno movie of a huge naked bald man having sex with a blow-up doll. Behind me I heard a cough and I spun around to see a wee tadpole of a man. He was naked and bald. Under other circumstances I might have said 'do us a favor mate and put that away'; instead I was telling myself to stay professional. I'm thinking what the hell am I doing? I'm in someone's apartment with who knows how many more naked bald fellows on the premises. But then I snapped out of it and he bought his grams of blow and that was the end of it. Soon as I got out I phoned the boss and told him thanks a lot you stupid prick, you might have given me the heads up, so to speak."

Cole's phone rang. "Karen, I'm downstairs. I'll be right there." He closed his phone, unsnapped his seat belt, and exited my car. "Thanks for the ride. I'm gonna need a drink after this."

Somewheresville

• • •

An unfinished
novella...

SOMEWHERESVILLE

The summer was over and I was, as the poets are wont to say, shit out of luck. Even my pot plants were dead.

After one full year at college in the north east I had repaired to a relaxing summer holiday at the home of my Uncle Archibald and Auntie Mildred near the beach, Somewheresville, south shore of Long Island, New York. This white clapboard with dark green trim colonial had been my home since I could remember.

It was the summer of hurricane Floyd and all over the news it was determined that the state of Florida was chewed up, and the entire country of Honduras would never be the same. What I knew empirically was that my feeble pubescent marijuana plants, outside on the porch, had perished in the storm and every time I saw ads for FEMA I contemplated petitioning for compensation on account of my crop failure.

I'd been home two weeks before I had gathered the courage to look the relatives square in the face and confess my decision. Rain had soaked the earth for two days solid and I remember it was a gloomy morning that found me and the relatives sitting in the blue and white themed breakfast nook. It was still early and a morning fog sat right outside the bay window, clouding things. We picked from a plate of fried sausages, which Auntie Mildred tenderly called 'bangers', as we did every Sunday; my aunt's idea of doffing the ancestral hat to Mother England. Max, the house dog, an enormous handsome mutt of murky origins kept himself discreetly under the table, where he lay on his side and methodically slapped the tip of his tail across the arch of my feet, a mild furry whip.

Tapping a banger at the edge of the plate, so that the grease pooled into a coagulation, I coughed and said, "what I learned at college, unequivocally, is that I have zero intention of wasting one more minute there. College, like it or not, is just a cushy jail delaying the inevitable. I'm not going back".

A monstrous battle ensued. Inexplicably my aunt held a sausage in each hand and was waving her arms around like a conductor at the opera, meanwhile murmuring, "…well I never! A person could have a heart attack!" a regular refrain from Auntie Mildred which generally preceded the ingestion of handfuls of 'calming' pills.

Uncle Archibald bashed the table with clenched fists but said nothing as he inelegantly wriggled his bulky torso free from the round table. Just as he had

168

himself standing upright somehow the plate of sausages began to wobble, as if possessed, and eerily slid to the floor. We all watched in horror, as if it were a portent of a bigger picture. The blue and white plate did not break when it hit the tiled floor, but instead sort of bounced and flipped over. The upshot of our fight was without a clear resolution on either side. All parties disbanded and the kitchen was soon vacant, except for Max, who set about scarfing the runaway sausages.

Despite more than forty years stateside Uncle Archibald and Auntie Mildred remained distinctly British; they studiously maintained their Queen's English, they belonged to a local bird watching society and they drank a lot of sherry. Another throwback to the motherland was their modus operandi of keeping a 'stiff upper lip'.

For the first few weeks of the summer holidays the relatives decided the best way to handle my "stubborn streak" was to ignore the matter. We three had gone some rounds before, through the years, and I was familiar with the routine.

"Gorgeous weather." Auntie Mildred said with her back to me, stirring baked beans in a pot on the stove. And then she wiped her twitchy fingers on the lace edge of her apron. "Could make a person want to do something with their lives."

I was lolling in a doorway, and I made a big point of crossing my arms and exhaling loudly. Max was always by my side, charmingly overprotective.

For most of his life Uncle Archibald had worked in the capacity of curator of the estate of an ex-pat English writer, claiming some far-flung blood connection by way of qualification. Had moved from his home on the south coast of England with his then young bride, to take the job.

"Lovely, Mildred, we don't say gorgeous. We say lovely, or splendid. Never gorgeous." Uncle Archibald's response was muffled by the newspaper he hid behind. While Uncle Archibald was not the funniest person I would ever know he was first-rate and his only visible weakness was gluttony. The pile-up of chins and corpulence was beyond portly.

He could have his newspaper, I thought, I have Max. Max was not fooled by the faux civility and he would press his whole body against me, and make fierce faces at the relatives. It was overkill, but very appealing.

Auntie Mildred was a traditional housewife content to fuss about the hearth, fry sausages on Sundays, and pad her nest with a dutiful devotion. Without fail every day Uncle Archibald went to work with a bag of sandwiches prepared for him the night before by Auntie Mildred. Punctilious, he was home by six in the evening, in time for a meal Auntie Mildred called "high tea", usually comprised of baked beans and towers of buttered toast, crusts off. Post repast the relatives liked to molder in upholstered armchairs, one on either side of a fire of pine cones, and read beagle hunting periodicals and sip Madeira sherry.

One morning Uncle Archibald, gathering his briefcase and his bag of sandwiches, ruled on my sentence, "No college, no free ride Lovie."

"No problem!" I spluttered, hoping to mask the shock I felt at the grotesque news.

"If you don't change your mind about school you'll need to move out by the end of the summer. Action Lovie, it's time for action."

I did nothing. For the rest of the summer I put the overambitious chore out of my mind. Instead I closed off and curled up in a hammock under the arched boughs of a Mulberry tree, where I read adventure books. Each tome convinced me more my own road in life should be the Gringo trail, the path of the traveler, the explorer.

Max was usually close by flopped on his side, snout ruffling as he growled in his sleep. I imagined he was dreaming of rabbits. Now the last days of August were upon me and time was evaporating. As a token gesture I scrolled the internet employment sites but inevitably I could not find anything agreeable. Either a dead chicken could get the job but the pay was low, or ridiculous quantities of years of 'experience' were required or no need applying. I'll admit I was disheartened.

In the evenings I would follow Max across the front yards and the back lawns of the homes of neighbors, meandering our way to the beach. Rabbits sprang about and Max devoted a lot of energy to trying to catch them. Chasing at full speed, carving corners low to the ground like a motorcycle, he got awfully close and I wouldn't mean to but sometimes I'd lose my nerve and yell at him to leave the defenseless bunnies be. Except that Max never caught a rabbit, which was a relief, although I couldn't help feeling embarrassed for him. He was cut like a body builder, he had speed like Ali, but he couldn't catch a bunny rabbit.

I threw some effort at the Web and conjured a television producer, one Mary Salt hell-bound on hiring an assistant, because, as she said, she was 'desperate'. She needed someone 'Pronto', no skills required. Show up at 12 tomorrow. A call to a pal with a guest room and I was good to go. I could scarcely believe how easy this all was. I couldn't restrain a pitying laugh when I thought of my former college-mates, clustered solemnly around the fount of knowledge, wasting time on theory when they could be out here in the world of practice.

The route from the beach to the middle of Manhattan is on average three hours. Reflexively I set up cruise control, reclined my seat and zoned out. My plan was to work only long enough to earn the funds to abscond and traipse the globe, until I turned twenty-five and received my inheritance. This tantalizing inheritance was a known quantity, but being as the relatives were Brits details were never discussed.

I was minding my own business in the center lane when I was startled by a blast. I snapped to attention to see something swirling rushing at me; it looked like a seal. Weirdly, it disappeared from sight. I searched in my rearview mirror but I could see no trace.

Up ahead a long haul truck switched on a stadium's worth of warning lights, flaring and flashing. A second explosion went off, and another seal flipped through the air.

Tires were disengaging from the truck's axle; bouncing haphazardly. A quick check of the flow of traffic and I dodged into the right lane. Vaguely I wondered what would happen to a car if it was to run over one of those tires.

My musings were interrupted by a man in a van. He had sidled up with a stricken look on his face. He was blaring his horn and pointing fingers at me. Oh go away, I thought and checked my watch, I'm on a schedule.

Next, a bus crammed with nuns in full black and white regalia slowed beside me and all of them were gesticulating, their faces vibrant with alarm.

What the hell? I negotiated to the shoulder of the highway, and parked.

I exited and met with a bad smell. I disregarded it, waving it off as a product of mid-Island over-population and took a look at my car. I could see nothing wrong. I walked around the back. Again, perfection, unless you count the crease in the bumper; a tree and a bad parking job. I was on the verge of concluding my inspection when I noticed an odd shape protruding from beneath the car, like a shark fin. I crouched to see most of a monster truck tire applied unevenly to the undercarriage of my automobile. A waft of stink stung my eyes, singed my nose. The tire was not on fire, but it was cooking up a nasty stench.

I tugged on it and it moved a fraction. I tugged some more, and it moved some more. It was slow going. Eventually, I was back on the road. I felt disgusting with sweat and a flushed hot face. It was less immediate that I noticed my hands were stained with sticky tar and much of it was already tie-dye-patterned down my blouse and my skirt. I was a wreck. I didn't even know how bad I was until compared to the spotless hi-tech sleek environs of the futuristic television executive offices.

Mahogany table, leather arm chairs, floor to ceiling plate glass windows with views of the stratosphere, and myself in Nascar-casual Friday pit-crew attire.

The double doors blasted open and in barreled a tiny dark haired lady. "Name's Mary Salt. Call me Mary," she said, spraying saliva. Stick thin, wobbling on six inch wedge shoes Mary was sporting a remarkable metal contraption on her head. Like a halo made of aerials it contoured her skull and entered her mouth like a horse bit.

"Late." Mary Salt remarked. She crossed her arms and stared, letting her eyes rove over me, "and you look like hell. This is not the way to make a good

175

impression on your new boss." Each word she spoke emerged in a bubble and then hung, in slimy drips, on the rungs of her metal headdress. She wobbled forward on the tottering shoes and just before what looked like an imminent fall she lurched into a chair. Her slender body landed with enough force to roll the chair into the side of the table, so that it shuddered. Once settled, Mary slung out a slim arm, extending her hand for me to shake. Her fingers were dry as winter twigs.

"In case you're wondering," Mary patted the bird cage around her head, "my dentist makes me wear this contraption." Mary sucked on the mouth bit, like a lizard panting between succulent mastications. She was awful to look at and I easily pictured myself running away. Instead, I handed over my resume. The typed words were in a huge font listing education, summer jobs, likes, dislikes and hobbies.

Mary took the resume in her hands, and as she read it she massaged the page with desiccated fingertips. And then she barked, spitting, "Is this a joke?"

I was stunned by her response. Nausea flooded my senses. In spite of desperately wanting to run all the way home, equally I had not considered rejection. After all, I had no contingency plan. "Please," I begged, "you don't understand, I really need this job. My whole life depends on..." I could not control my voice from cracking.

"Your name is Santa? For real? And what's with the phony Brit accent? Is that for my benefit?" Mary's narrow frame began to shake and she started to guffaw, hee- hawing like a donkey.

I took a deep breath, steadying myself for the audition of a lifetime, "my full name is Santa Maria Astral Smith-Hawthorne." Heart rattling, I felt I was clawing my way back from some invisible brink. "I'm American, born on Long Island, but I was raised by a very English aunt and uncle. It's complicated."

"Whatever!" Mary crushed my resume into a ball and lobbed it over her shoulder. "Follow me." She commanded and darted from the room.

Down a corridor and through a constant spray of drool Mary chattered, moving surprisingly fast on her towering shoes and I had to hasten my gait to keep up. "Office supplies in there." Mary flicked a hand toward an open door we sped by. "Over here is the copy room. You know how to use a copy machine?"

"Of course!" I said. In truth I did not, but now was not the time to divulge trifles.

"Pay is six hundred dollars a week, not including taxes, and I'll give you vouchers for the cafeteria on the fifth floor." Mary outlined the duties of my job as her assistant and she explained how I would very likely become frustrated because my responsibilities

177

would be rote while her own job, a developer of childrens television programming, was scintillating. Spinning her wedding band around her finger, Mary said, "I'm a lucky lady, great husband, great kid, great job…" Mary droned on and I spaced out, that is until I heard her say, "…in about six months you can look forward to developing projects of your own.…' Mary paused and winked at me, saliva-spume twinkling.

Six months, I laughed to myself, while conveying nothing of my thoughts, in six months I'll be long gone. Six months from now I hope to be irretrievably lost somewhere down the path of adventure.

Having fully circumnavigated the eleventh floor Mary and I were now standing in the foyer. "Consider yourself hired. I expect you here at ten sharp tomorrow morning. Get your parking ticket validated by the receptionist."

The reception area was an oval in shades of beige, with a desk dead center. The man at the desk was talking on the telephone so I leaned against a wall and waited. The man was big and soft, young yet balding. The man was speaking softly, his torso was curled forward and hunched. But his words were just loud enough that I couldn't help but eavesdrop. "I love you too," he was murmuring, "I love you more," he cajoled and then delicately hung up the phone.

"Sorry to bother you Mr. uh… Cannelloni?" as I approached I quickly glanced at the name plaque conveniently placed at the lip of the table 'Gianfranco Canneleoni'.

"Pain in the ass!" The man shouted, and as he did so he picked up the telephone receiver and slammed it hard several times into the cradle. "It's Canne-LEO-ni. My mother calls me Gianni. You can call me John." He smiled at me and the furrows on his brow relaxed. As he spoke he took my parking ticket and thumped it with a rubber stamp. "That was my girlfriend I was talking to. We're getting married soon and she's all freaked out. Pain in the ass!"

Emma, a girl I knew from college, offered up the use of her fuchsia moiré satin sofa, "for a week or so, until you find a place of your own." Emma's trust fund took care of the details of her comfortable life. This included the ground floor of a townhouse on the Upper East Side. Half way along a leafy side street, down one step to a sunken courtyard the heavy front door was couched beneath a stone archway. This opened to a living room of oversized furniture in shades of Gothic and blood, and in an alcove the fuchsia moiré satin sofa now converted to my bed. From the living room a corridor with kitchen and bathroom to either side and in the back one enormous bedroom with a fireplace and a four poster bed laden with frilly pillows, and trays of soiled crockery and upturned egg shells filled with a thousand cigarette ends. Beyond a set of French doors was a petite garden, with a wrought iron bench and an actual grass lawn the size of a bathmat.

I did not see much of Emma, and since I could hear her television constantly on I imagined she lounged in bed all day. Emma was not a talker, and her reputation at college was that she was a little 'slow'. Occasionally, often after I was tucked in on the sofa, Emma would slink out into the night, all dressed up in fancy clothes. She never said goodbye. When I left for work in the morning I presumed she was returned to her four poster bed, but I did not think to check. In spite of her hospitality her existence scarcely scratched my consciousness. In any case, she could not compete for entertainment value with the sights I saw on my daily jaunt to and from work.

Like the guy in a green tutu and high heels and full on make-up, his well defined solid ass muscles gyrating out there for all to see. Or the little old lady, in an electric chair, speeding in amongst the taxicabs down the center lane of Fifth Avenue, a male nurse chasing, hollering. My commute entailed twenty minutes of zigzagging from the Upper East Side to the axis of bedlam, otherwise known as Times Square. Each day I passed a schoolyard, half a block of cement and basketball hoops with no nets. In the morning it teemed with boisterous small kids, hunchbacked by book bags. And in the evenings, on my walk home the courtyard was empty on the school side, but on the street side of the chain link fence lingered a throng of men in hooded sweatshirts and baggy jeans and peacock flora sneakers. They were always there, and when I walked by them they hissed: "Sess, sess, sess."

For the first few days of this I was keenly terrified and kept my sights trained on the ground and scurried by them. But after a while my curiosity was tickled. One evening, coming up on the gang I stopped, and asked, "What the hell is 'Sess'?"

"Sessamilia." They burst into a chorus.

"What the hell?"

"Watch your language," said the tallest and widest of the group. He then took it upon himself to explain his was a marijuana outfit and that he and his men owned that particular corner. He flashed me a wad of cash from his pocket. Some of his cohorts also pulled out rolls of bills.

"Can I work with you?" I asked, semi-serious.

"This work is for men." The tall wide man began, and then he stirred with righteousness and doled out a lecture with threads along the lines of what did I think I was doing walking around in the evening by myself at my age? And on he sermonized. This was not what I had expected from New York City. I was so stunned I meekly took the scolding. At least now I had a supplier. Nights I began letting myself into Emma's bedroom, to access the garden, and the wrought iron bench upon which to sit and smoke a joint. I was tiptoeing through her room for some time before I noticed the mass of flotsam on the bed was not Emma. Thus I learned she did not always return from her nocturnal forays.

It was soon apparent I did not possess Mary's instincts for genius in children's entertainment. Work, such as it was called, amounted to reading an incessant influx of unsolicited scripts. Topics favored the supernatural, and all were laced with syrupy morality messages. Where Mary saw magic I saw putrefaction. My job was to read and reduce these scripts to one hundred word reports. So like school, I marveled. I was printing out my latest report, one hundred words meant to eviscerate a script about a 'good' pirate, when I heard:

"Yoo-hoo!" Mary screamed from her office. By now fully on automatic, I eased from my chair to the doorway of her office in a single fluid motion.

"I want the first banquette at Mondiale for twelve-thirty and then confirm the reservation with Pig." Chomping on her headpiece she handed me a scrap of notepaper with the word 'Pig' and a phone number.

For all of Mary's eccentricities, she had a spotless track record producing hits. She claimed she had a formula for auguring, and amazingly, she was always right, one saccharine children's brain-rot after another. I had already figured out her secret formula. She passed everything by Willow, her eight year old daughter.

Mary brought Willow to work some days and gave me the odious task of escorting the small child to the bathroom when the need arose, and the need arose all day long.

Back at my desk I phoned Mary's favorite bistro and reserved the booth for two near the front door. I was feeling like I was definitely getting the hang of things. It was going to be alright after all. Just do my time and presto! Travel and hammocks forever. Before Mary left for lunch I maternally retrieved the iron scaffold from her head.

Down the hall, in a small room filled with machines, the printer was retching a piece of paper. I pulled on the page and got squirted in the chest with ink.

"Cannelloni." I whispered as loudly as I dared into

the intercom.

"Canne-LEO-LEO-LEO-ni." He sounded exasperated.

"Help! Copy room."

In moments I heard the sounds of Cannelloni's bulk lumbering along the hallway and I felt a twinge of embarrassment as the formerly noble printer was reduced to beeping and grinding.

Like a detective come upon a crime scene Cannelloni loomed and coolly absorbed the evidence. He read the clues expertly and crossed the room to the bucking printer. He flicked open a plastic panel and extracted a tumor of crumpled pages. "I'm selling two tickets to the ballgame this Saturday. It's the fiancé's birthday and she wants me to take her to the mall and then out to dinner. I hate going to restaurants with her. She's always telling me I'm too fat, and she doesn't let me eat anything. She's a pain in the ass."

I took my ruined documents and dropped them into a plastic tub labeled 'Recycle'. "I don't get it Cannelloni Why are you with this girl? You're always complaining about her."

"What can I say? She's got great tits."

I returned to my cubicle and lazily rolled back in the comfortable office chair, and fell fast asleep.

"Yoo-hoo!" Mary's voice pierced some intense dream of a beach and a storm and something to do with running. "Santa!" Mary continued to shriek so that the sound scooped me up and had me standing at attention before I was even fully awake.

"How was lunch?" I asked, gathering myself.

"I can't understand it. I waited an hour at the restaurant and Pig never showed up!" Mary prattled while she bolted on her head gear and began to slurp on the mouth bit.

From nowhere, a blast of radiation, I knew what had happened. "Ah, um," I began, the searing heat of clarity microwaving me as I realized I would surely be fired. Reluctantly, I pointed to Mary's office and said, "I am so sorry, Mary, you might want to sit down for this." Single file we trooped in and took our positions across from one another at her immense desk.

"What's with your shirt?" Mary stared at me, her eyes wide with wonderment.

I looked down to see the printer fluid had stained a patch of my blouse. "That's another story." I said, and cleared my throat, "I never phoned your friend, Mr. Pig. I guess I forgot. I'm really sorry."

Mary eyed me, the tip of her tongue flicking against her mouthful of metal, and then she heaved forward and exploded with the laughter of a pack of hyenas. She spluttered until tears gushed from her eyes.

"Everyone makes mistakes." She said, and she dabbed at the brine with a tissue.

...TO BE CONTINUED

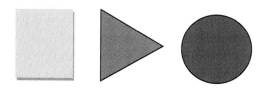

...CONGRATULATIONS! YOU MADE IT TO...

THE END

About the Author

Christina Oxenberg was born, and briefly raised, in New York City. This was followed by prolonged stays in London, then Madrid, then back to New York before returning to London, and so on, until after 14 schools and a multitudinous array of stepparents and their tribes of offspring, a precedent for adventure was set.

Bypassing university, Oxenberg plunged into a whirlpool of random employment, everything from researcher to party organizer to art dealer to burger flipper.

Oxenberg's single true love is writing, and she published her first book, TAXI, a collection of anecdotes about the adventures that can be had in the back seat of New York City taxicabs, in 1986. Despite the lousy pay, Oxenberg published articles in Allure Magazine, The London Sunday Times Magazine, Tattler, Salon.com, Penthouse and anyone else who would have her.

In 2000, Oxenberg was seduced by the offer of a regular paycheck and she fell down the rabbit-hole world of fine fibers. In the blink of an eye, a decade vanished into an unwieldy wool business. With relief, she returns to the relative calm of writing.

Between excursions, Oxenberg lives in Key West, Florida.

Photograph by Leigh Vogel©
www.leighvogel.com

For press, speaking engagements and other inquires
contact:

Ox Press
PO Box 1534
Key West Florida 33041

Website: www.wooldomination.com
Email: wooldomination@gmail.com

Printed in Great Britain
by Amazon

82910834R00111